MW00477602

Pure Survival

Tactics and Techniques to Help You Survive in the Wild

Samuel T. Heart

© Copyright 2020 - All rights reserved.

The content contained within this book may not be reproduced, duplicated, or transmitted without direct written permission from the author or the publisher.

Under no circumstances will any blame or legal responsibility be held against the publisher, or author, for any damages, reparation, or monetary loss due to the information contained within this book, either directly or indirectly.

Legal Notice:

This book is copyright protected. It is only for personal use. You cannot amend, distribute, sell, use, quote, or paraphrase any part, or the content within this book, without the consent of the author or publisher.

Disclaimer Notice:

Please note the information contained within this document is for educational and entertainment purposes only. All effort has been executed to present accurate, up to date, reliable, complete information. No warranties of any kind are declared or implied. Readers acknowledge that the author is not engaged in the rendering of legal, financial, medical, or professional advice. The content within this book has been derived from various sources. Please consult a licensed professional before attempting any techniques outlined in this book.

By reading this document, the reader agrees that under no circumstances is the author responsible for any losses, direct or indirect, that are incurred as a result of the use of the information contained within this document, including, but not limited to, errors, omissions, or inaccuracies.

Table of Contents

INTRODUCTION 1

    ABOUT THE AUTHOR 3

CHAPTER 1: THE GREAT OUTDOORS 5

    HISTORY OF BUSHCRAFT 5
    WHAT IS BUSHCRAFT ALL ABOUT? 6
    WHO IS INTERESTED IN BUSHCRAFT? 7
        Fun and Adventure 7
        Family Bonding 8
        School Bushcraft Camps 8
        Company Team Building 9
        Preppers/Survivalists 10
        Sense of Freedom 10
        Environmentalists 11
        Achievement, Reward, and Value 11
    WOOD IS A NECESSITY OF LIFE 11
        Splitting Wood 12
        Cutting Across the Wood Grain 12
        Cutting With the Grain 13
        Shaping Wood 13
        Wood Boring 13
    GETTING INTO PHYSICAL SHAPE IS ESSENTIAL 14
    SAFETY AND HEALTH IS TOP PRIORITY 15
        Human Waste Disposal 16
        Personal Hygiene 16
        Food Prep and Storage 17
    WATER 19
    PRACTICE MAKES PERFECT 19
    LOOK AFTER THE LAND 21
    THE ATTITUDE OF A SURVIVALIST 23
        Accept Easy Wins 24

Recognize and Accept Situations 24
Adapt to Changes 25
Avoid Unnecessary Risks 25
Conserve Your Energy 26
Get Creative and Improvise 26
Humor 27
Strong Work Ethic 27
Persistence, Resolve, and Endurance 28
Positive Attitude 29

CHAPTER 2: MODERN TOOLS FOR PRIMITIVE LIVING 31

CLOTHES 32
Gloves 33
Two Hats 33
Hiking Boots 34
Pants for the Outdoors 34
Socks 35
T-Shirts 36
Undergarments 36
Heavy Warm Outer Layer 36
Lightweight Warm Tops 37
Waterproof Garments 37
ESSENTIAL BUSHCRAFT TOOLS 38
The Sharp Edges 38

CHAPTER 3: THE POWER OF BEING YOUR OWN ARCHITECT . 49

ROPE CRAFT 49
Why is Rope Craft Important? 49
Tying Knots 51
BASIC WILDERNESS SHELTERS 52
Location is Key 53
Choose Your Spot 54
BUILDING MATERIALS FOR SHELTERS 56
Solid frame Shelters 56
Materials for Roofing 57
Ground Cover 57
Shelter-Building Tools 58
DIFFERENT SHELTERS FOR DIFFERENT NEEDS 59

COCOON OR DEBRIS SHELTER FOR EMERGENCIES............................ 60
TARP SHELTERS FOR EMERGENCIES OR CONVENIENCE 61
Tarp Wedge 61
Tarp Wedge A-Frame Shelter 62
Tarp Tent Shelter 64
Tarp Wing Shelter... 64
Tarp Burrito Shelter 65
Lean-To Tarp Shelter... 67
LEAN-TO SHELTERS.. 67
SEMI-PERMANENT SHELTERS.. 69
A-FRAME SHELTERS... 69
Basic/Classic A-Frame.. 70
Tree-Supported A-Frame 72
Wedge A-Frame Shelter.. 73
QUINZHEE SNOW SHELTERS 74
Snow Shelter Dangers.. 74
Quinzhee Shelter Design 75
Quinzhee Tips... 77

CHAPTER 4: GET YOUR GAME ON 79

HUNTING... 79
The Importance of a Good Knife 80
Weapon Considerations.. 81
Consider Your Prey.. 82
Consider Your Skills.. 83
The Importance of Primitive Hunting Techniques............ 85
Hunting Tips.. 86
TRACKING 88
What is Animal Tracking?... 89
Tracks vs. Signs 90
Why is Tracking Important? 90
Characteristics of Reading Tracks..................................... 91
Tracking Signs That Are Not Tracks 94
Seeing Tracks in More Detail 95
Do Your Research... 96
TRAPPING 97
Trapping: Advantages and Disadvantages...................... 97
Types of Traps.. 99

Where to Set Traps and Snares 104
Decommission Traps and Snares 105
Caution 105
FISHING.. 106
Making Your Own Fishing Hooks..................................... 107
Making Your Own Fishing Line 108
Making Your Own Fishing Rod... 108
Finding Bait.. 109
Spearfishing 110
COOKING MEAT AND FISH 112
Preparing Game for Cooking 113
Preparing Fish for Cooking 114

CHAPTER 5: FORAGE FOR FOOD AND MEDICINE................. 117

TIPS FOR LEARNING TO FORAGE 118
TIPS FOR ACTIVELY FORAGING 120
GETTING STARTED.. 122
MEDICINAL PLANTS 124
UNIVERSAL EDIBILITY TEST 126

CHAPTER 6: WATER, THE SOURCE OF LIFE 129

WHY IS WATER SO IMPORTANT?... 130
Signs of Dehydration 132
Severity of Dehydration 132
Conserving Body Fluids 133
FINDING WATER AND COLLECTING IT 134
WATER SAFETY.. 137
Making Water Potable 139

CHAPTER 7: THE STORY OF A SPINDLE AND A BOARD......... 145

NOT ALL WOOD IS EQUAL 145
Which Wood to Burn 149
Tips for Efficient Wood Burning...................................... 151
Avoid Wet Wood 152
Finding Seasoned Wood 152
Wood to Avoid... 153
STARTING A FIRE 155
Starting a Fire Au Natural... 155

Other Ways to Start a Fire *158*

KEEPING A FIRE GOING... 160

FIRE SAFETY 160

CHAPTER 8: BE READY FOR THE UNEXPECTED 163

EXTREME COLD.. 163

Storm Tips.. *164*

EXTREME HEAT.. 164

LIGHTNING.. 165

FLOODING 167

NAVIGATION 168

Common Compass Mistakes.. *169*

No Map or Compass? *170*

Finding North Without a Compass *172*

When You're Lost.. *174*

FIRST AID 175

CPR.. *176*

Splint Making.. *176*

Cleaning and Dressing Wounds *177*

Treating Shock *177*

Stemming Bleeding... *178*

Treating Hypothermia *178*

Treating Hyperthermia *180*

Burn Treatment *180*

CONCLUSION.. 181

REFERENCES... 183

Introduction

"The man, who goes afoot, prepared to camp anywhere and in any weather,

is the most independent fellow on earth."

-by Dave Canterbury

"I am prepared for the worst, but hope for the best." – Benjamin Disraeli

Bushcraft and survival go hand-in-hand when you enjoy an outdoor lifestyle. It encompasses various essential survival skills so that, should you find yourself in a sticky situation in the wilderness, you are prepared to make the most of it. Being able to draw on this knowledge and skill set will go a long way to helping you survive in an emergency situation. Not only that, but they are also fun to learn and practice.

Many people want to enjoy an escape from the big city in a modern world that is constantly bustling and driven by technology. There is just something about the great outdoors that awakens a primal desire to embrace a lifestyle that includes regular periods spent surrounded by the almost untouched natural world. This is great!

However, it does come with responsibility. It is your responsibility to ensure that you aren't left "up a creek without a paddle," so to speak. This is where bushcraft for survival comes in. Having the knowledge, tools, and skills to survive will ease any uncertainty that city slickers may have about venturing out into the great unknown, which allows them to more thoroughly enjoy their time in nature.

Not only is bushcraft advantageous for survival in the face of adversity. It is also a set of skills that is fun to learn and share with friends and family. You don't have to be in a survival situation to build a shelter, create primitive ways of starting a fire, or learn to navigate without a GPS. These are skills that you can teach your children while spending quality time together. You can pass on invaluable knowledge while having fun and nurturing a love of nature.

Some of what you can expect to learn from this book includes:

- Essential bushcraft tools and supplies.
- How to build basic shelters.
- How to fish with the bare minimum.
- How to navigate using the sun and stars.
- How to be self-reliant in getting yourself out of a tricky situation.
- And much more.

All of these skills draw on the knowledge and skills passed down through generations of our ancestors.

Most people in modern society have lost this knowledge and the skills that go with it. Now is your chance to embrace the wilderness, return to a more natural space away from the humdrum of the city, and enjoy being more in tune with an untamed, wild environment. If that sounds like it's just what you want and need, keep reading.

About the Author

Samuel is an outdoor enthusiast. Having lived in the countryside much of his life, he embraces the love of wild spaces. As a kid, Samuel would go on long camping trips with his father, learning the bushcraft skills and gaining the insight and knowledge of being out in the wilderness from his father, who had learned them from his father. The knowledge had been passed down through generations and came to Samuel as a kind of intangible family heirloom.

When Samuel moved to the city to attend college and start working, he left the countryside behind but never lost the love of nature or the desire to experience it. Nature was a part of him and he could never stay away long. On one of these regular camping trips, friends joined. They urged Samuel to teach them some of the bushcraft skills he knew so much about, both for recreation and survival. It was a fantastic success. His friends were hooked, they embraced the wild and couldn't get enough of learning how to handle themselves in the outdoors.

After that camping trip with friends, Samuel had found his true calling. He would do what he loved most. He would become a survival coach and share his knowledge with clients who wanted to learn how to be more in tune with nature and how to make the most of their time outdoors, but also how to be prepared for unforeseen events. He draws on his lifetime of experience honing his natural bushcraft skills and he's turned his passion into a career.

Samuel is a successful survival coach, a husband, and the father of a bright young boy whom he loves to share his knowledge and skills with on camping trips. He also knows that it's not possible to teach everyone who wants to learn bushcraft in person and that is why this book was written. Samuel wants to be able to share some of his knowledge with a wider audience so that they too can begin their journey in bushcraft and outdoor survival. He wants to share that knowledge with you so keep on reading to pick up some of that vast knowledge and apply it to your own outdoor adventures.

Chapter 1:

The Great Outdoors

Our world runs on technology and many people cannot imagine a world without the things they take for granted. For them life without smartphones, Wi-Fi, airplanes, credit cards, and everything at hand with the push of a button is inconceivable. Technology is not bad or evil, yet others yearn to reconnect with humanity's roots and get back to nature.

History of Bushcraft

The words bushcraft and survivalism are popular and used by various groups and individuals today who want to learn and practice the skills of living in the wilderness. The concept though is not new at all. For millennia bushcraft was how our ancestors survived their daily lives. If you did not have the necessary skills to survive in the wilderness, you simply did not survive.

Bushcraft is in fact the history of the human species. As we progressed to villages and later to towns and cities, the skills for survival in the wilderness faded into the background until it became stories people would tell their children.

What Is Bushcraft All About?

Bushcraft is about learning and practicing the skills that will allow you to survive in the wilderness—to live without all the modern conveniences most people in the 21st century deem to be basic necessities.

It means that you must learn how to make a shelter to protect you from the elements and whatever animals are out there. Then follows the skills from finding food to sustain yourself—which includes foraging, hunting, or trapping animals—to how to purify water to enable you to have clean drinking water. You also need to learn to deal with injuries and what to treat them with, and what to use to keep the bugs away as well as how to treat stings and bites.

All of this may seem overwhelming at first but that is only because we have moved so far from our roots that we have forgotten a great deal. The good news, however, is that you have time to learn the skills you need over a period of time and it becomes easier with every step you take forward.

Who Is Interested in Bushcraft?

This question does not have a short, simple answer for wilderness skills that are sought by many different groups and individuals for reasons that suit their personal needs. Therefore, asking this question of 10 different people will most likely give you 10 very different answers.

Whatever their personal reasons are, people interested in bushcraft want to relearn the skills to survive and thrive in nature. To be able to interact with nature and survive on the bounty that mother nature provides in abundance.

Fun and Adventure

People who grow up in cities want to learn the skills of how to forage, hunt, fish, and live off the land, as it is the complete opposite of the lives they are used to. Every time they master a new bushcraft skill they experience a great sense of achievement in having learned a useful skill that they had known nothing about before. The reward for them is being able to have and use skills that the majority of people around them simply have no idea about. Mastering these skills adds value to their lives on many different levels.

Family Bonding

Learning bushcraft skills as a family brings families closer together. It reinforces the bond when children not only learn new skills but also see their parents doing this with them. Parents also provide a solid foundation for their children to learn to understand and value nature. This is a gift from a parent to their children that has a positive impact on children into their adult lives. The lessons and skills they learn as children give them a different perspective of the world that could lead to different career choices and what they value throughout their lives.

School Bushcraft Camps

Schools have come to realize the value of taking kids to bushcraft survival camps, as the benefits of teaching children bushcraft skills not only equipes them with new skills but it gives children confidence in themselves. They learn that there is a world out there where technology and computers have no place and they can have fun without that. Children also learn valuable lessons about working together in a team to achieve goals. Another benefit is that there is not only one type of bushcraft camp or course for children. There is a wide variety of courses that are age-appropriate and camps that focus on specific topics, therefore parents can choose what they feel is the most appropriate for their child.

Company Team Building

Companies today face many challenges in an ever-changing financial climate. To stay competitive they need to motivate their staff to work together. Bushcraft camps and classes have become a very popular alternative to the traditional team building that did not take people out of their comfort zones. What makes teaching employees and teams survival skills so unique is that everyone is taken out of their comfort zones. Far away from the office, business suits, and computers. People see their colleagues in a totally different environment and everyone is exposed to a completely new experience. These team-building events can be tailored to suit specific needs and people can spend a day in the wilderness or longer periods of time. People bond where before they were distant from colleagues and they learn survival skills and empathy as well.

Many people feel confined and shackled by our modern lifestyle with its sedative lifestyle of office and home. They find the adventure that they feel their lives lack through learning and practicing survival skills, and they have a huge amount of fun taking wilderness trips and living off the land. It is the therapy they need to balance their need for adventure and their careers in modern surroundings.

Preppers/Survivalists

Preppers, also called survivalists, are not people who seem a bit strange and run around stockpiling everything in sight for an imaginary emergency or disaster. Preppers are serious about being prepared for emergency situations in the future. These could be natural disasters and surviving extreme weather conditions that may cut them off from civilization. Bushcraft skills form part of the prepper lifestyle whether the disasters are natural or manmade.

These skills will allow them to survive and be safe, and also teach them how to deal with certain medical emergencies when they cannot get to a doctor or a hospital. Being prepared and having learned survival skills can save your life or the life of another person.

Sense of Freedom

Bushcraft and survival skills give people a chance to closely interact with nature on a scale that is not possible when camping out with all the modern camping equipment available. You move from being an observer of nature to being part of nature and your environment. You gain freedom from depending on modern conveniences and with survival skills you only depend on yourself.

Environmentalists

Learning survival skills is important to survivalists in their goal to protect our natural environment from the many ways humans are destroying our natural surroundings. These skills allow them to interact with nature without leaving traces of human activity behind.

Achievement, Reward, and Value

People are attracted to learning and practicing bushcraft, and they want to pit the survival skills they have learned against nature as it gives them a great sense of achievement. They strive to learn and master skills that are very different from the skills needed in their daily lives. Mastering these skills is the reward that they seek and each new skill they master is a huge achievement for them. They feel that these skills add value to their lives. Survivalists often explain that practicing these skills makes them feel more alive than they feel in their modern, daily lives.

Wood Is a Necessity of Life

From the earliest times in human history, wood has been an integral part of survival. Wood is an incredible renewable source used in just about everything when you live in the wilderness.

Versatile uses wood for survival depends on your own creativity, but the following are the basic uses:

- Fire for cooking and heat.
- To build shelters.
- Make weapons for hunting and defense, such as bows and arrows.
- Medicine and first aid, using the bark, resin, and sap.
- Carving of utensils like cups, spoons, plates, forks, and bowls.

When you start out as a beginner in bushcraft you need to know the five basic ways to process wood with simple tools. Each of the five different processing ways gives the best results for specific tasks and uses.

Splitting Wood

This is the most basic way of cutting wood, by splitting it into logs for firewood. Several tools can be used, with an ax being the usual first option.

Cutting Across the Wood Grain

You will use this method for cutting wood to obtain long ridge poles for making the roof and frame for bush shelters, and also for center poles for tents.

Cutting With the Grain

Cutting wood with the grain creates your strongest timber and logs so this is your most versatile cut of all and you also use this cut when you intend shaping the wood.

Shaping Wood

Shaping the wood means you cut it to have level lengths and flat or smooth edges. Whereas you can cut across the grain if you want crude and simple poles, for anything that requires smooth or flat edges you need to cut with the grain such as lumber and bows.

Wood Boring

Boring through the wood is done when you need precision sized holes, and you need specialized tools for this as the wrong tools can ruin the wood for its intended use.

Getting Into Physical Shape Is Essential

Physical fitness is an often overlooked facet of bushcraft and survival practice. People often assume that they are in okay shape as they are used to mild exercise, or they go to the gym. There is a huge difference between being an urban fit and wilderness fit.

The differences are:

- Uneven terrain, mountain trails with steep inclines, and traversing rocks and waterways that require dexterity and using muscles that you may not be using regularly.
- Carrying a heavy load of equipment.
- The need for increased strength and endurance without muscle fatigue setting in and draining your strength.
- You cannot stop after an hour as you would at the gym, you must be fit enough to continue to the location you are aiming for.
- A sufficient diet to sustain your muscles and stamina during long wilderness hikes.

Getting your body into shape is where you start to enable yourself to do all the tasks that are necessary on a daily basis to live in the wilderness. You need to prep a minimum of eight weeks before you want to go on your first survival camp. There are numerous free fitness plans available on the internet to specifically get you into shape for survival. Download a suitable fitness plan and guideline that suits your personal needs and start out on the right foot with this new journey you want to embark on. Being wilderness fit will keep you safe and prevent accidents due to your body not being able to cope.

Safety and Health Is Top Priority

Taking survival trips usually has the goal of getting away from it all. Remove yourself from the stress that modern life puts on everybody and the strain we all experience trying to cope with a world that just keeps moving faster. To be able to enjoy reconnecting to nature and the environment should be a positive experience and a lot of fun. If, however, you do not take basic safety and personal hygiene measures that you will have to deal with in the wilderness, things can go wrong with unpleasant consequences.

You have to think outside the box about things that you take for granted in our modern society and have the solutions at hand.

Human Waste Disposal

Safety starts with disposing of human waste. You should choose a toilet site downstream, as well as downwind from the site where you make camp. This is an important safety measure so that smells do not attract animals to your campsite and waste will not be carried towards your camp. The trench or pit should be adequate for the time you will spend there, plus the number of people using it. Once the trench is no longer needed, dispose of any used paper by burning it and throwing the ashes into the trench before completely covering the trench with soil. Always mark the toilet site by placing crossed sticks on top to alert others to not use that specific spot for a loo trench. The waste will compost over time and not be a hazard to humans or animals.

Personal Hygiene

Keeping your body clean and making sure you wash your hands before and after handling food is vital to ensure that harmful bacteria cannot cross-contaminate food. It is not difficult to make a canvas bucket shower, and it is perfect for keeping clean physically. It is important because any scrapes and scratches you get can become infected much easier in the wilderness. Make sure that you choose your shower site away from any watercourses to prevent contamination of a much-needed water supply.

Food Prep and Storage

We take fridges, freezers, running water, garbage disposals, and kitchen cupboards that close securely for granted in our lives. All that falls away in the wilderness. You have to find other solutions for keeping your food secure from animals, keeping food fresh, and ensuring no bacterial cross-contamination takes place. Bad storage and lax hygiene practices will lead to interaction with animals you did not want, and health hazards, including diarrhea and vomiting, from eating contaminated food.

This sounds rather doom and gloom but being practical when out in the wilderness stops things going wrong. All it takes is preparing well and following some easy and simple rules with your food, the preparation thereof, and storing it properly.

- When you work with food, make sure that you wash your hands before you start.
- Keep the food as clean as is practically possible, especially meat, to prevent contamination.
- Make sure you prepare food on a clean surface. If at all possible carry a lightweight cutting board with you to work on. This will prevent the chance of the food coming into contact with any surfaces that may be contaminated.
- Cook all meat thoroughly as a safety measure. When cooking meat to be rare, the internal temperature of the meat does not reach 165

degrees F, which is the temperature at which bacteria die.

- After use, clean all kitchen utensils very well and put them into a container to keep them safe from contamination until you use them again.

- Store all food off the ground so that animals cannot get to it. If possible use a container that is small animal-proof such as badgers, rats, squirrels, and mice. Rodents can seriously damage your equipment and they will contaminate the food that they do not eat with bacteria clinging to their paws and fur.

- Never leave any food waste around your campsite as it will attract insects, flies, and other animals.

- Dispose of kitchen waste in your campfire and bury any residue.

- Dispose of any grey water away from your campsite by pouring it out. The ground will filter the water before it reaches any water source.

- To keep your food cool wet a large piece of cotton material and drape it over your food. As the water evaporates it keeps the food at a cooler temperature than the surrounding temperature.

Water

It is not possible to know whether water is safe to drink by simply looking at it. You have to purify and/or filter the water to ensure your safety. Remember that when you are in a tight spot, you can make a make-shift filter bag from the clothes that you have on hand. Look through your clothes and whatever item you have that has the closest weave, that is the one to use as a filter. (See Chapter 6 for detailed information about the importance of water and the various ways to purify water to make it safe to drink).

Practice Makes Perfect

We learn from the moment we are born and keep learning throughout our lives; there is always something new to learn, to experience, and it is part of learning survival skills to read about the various aspects of survival skills. Keep the book handy for reference and to refresh your memory.

Nobody can expect to get into the driver's seat of a car for the first time and when the car is started to automatically be a Formula 1 driver. Skills take practice and more practice and that is what every person starting out learning bushcraft has to do. You cannot just head off into the wilderness with a backpack; you need to first master all the necessary skills for survival by attending courses that will prepare you for the wilderness.

There are survival courses available to suit everyone, from total beginners that can attend day and overnight classes to month-long courses for the more experienced. Look at what is available on the internet and then pick the classes that suit your circumstances, level of skills, and experience or lack thereof.

Extra benefits, besides learning survival skills, you will get from attending classes are:

- You get the opportunity to practice and hone your skills in a setting that does not put your life at risk.

- You experience group dynamics as you will be working with people from different backgrounds, various experience levels, and work in a group with people who can be annoying, stubborn, distracting, and who are whiners and moaners. You will learn to handle it all to make the group function smoothly.

- You experience being totally out of your comfort zone where you can't press buttons to get what you want. You learn patience as you cannot call for pizza delivery, you have to make the food yourself and the reward is the sense of achievement you get from being able to take care of your needs yourself.

- You learn life skills that you need to use in your everyday life such as making decisions in adverse conditions and handling yourself under stress.

Look After the Land

Humans are messy. Yes, that is a generalization, as there are countless people who are conscious of the impact they have on the environment, but far too many people have become self-entitled. This perception that they deserve the privilege to mess wherever they wish with no consequences is the reason our oceans are drowning in garbage. Our pristine wilderness areas are incredibly important and for everybody to be prepared to leave no traces of their passing when they are out there hiking, camping, or on a wilderness trek.

The Leave No Trace ethic has been adopted and advocated by various organizations, including the U.S. Forestry Service. This wilderness ethic started in the mid-20th-century and has grown over the years in the efforts to conserve our wilderness areas and to protect the animals and their habitats.

The concept of Leave No Trace is based on seven principles that everyone who goes out there to practice bushcraft and survival skills need to adhere to for the protection of the environment and the animal kingdom.

These seven principles are:

- Always plan everything before you go and make sure you know the regulations that cover the specific area you are going to be in. Plan for any emergencies such as weather changes and injuries.

- Show respect to all the wildlife that you encounter. Never interact with the animals and definitely never feed them, and minimize the impact you have on ecosystems.

- Minimize the impact your campfires have on the environment by only making the fire for the purpose you will be using it for. You do not need a bonfire to cook food and make very sure each time you make a fire you burn it completely to ashes.

- Practice sensible waste management as discussed under safety and health in this chapter. It is important to remember that waste you cannot dispose of properly on the spot must be carried back with you to be disposed of at home.

- Leave anything from nature where you found it. Never bring keepsakes back with you and make sure you dismantle anything you have built at your campsite.

- Choose your campsite as discussed under safety and health to minimize your impact on the environment without disturbing animal habitats.
- Follow hiking etiquette by showing respect and consideration to any other visitors you come across, or others you know are in the same general area as you are. Stand aside when you encounter a pack animal on the path you are on and always allow other hikers to pass. Also, be quiet when out in the wilderness to minimize your impact on any visitors to the area and the animals who live there.

The Attitude of a Survivalist

What makes a person a survivalist? It takes more than having the right equipment and having done some bushcraft courses. The best-laid plans can go astray and if you have not cultivated the mindset and attitude of a survivalist, then things may not always end well. When you find yourself in the wilderness or in an emergency situation, you need more than equipment, and being reckless and overconfident has no place in survival. When you have a survival mentality you can get through most natural and manmade disasters and emergencies.

Accept Easy Wins

Accept what is offered easily in the wilderness. There is no need to try and impress anyone with your stalking skills—take the easy shot, and be happy with it. Trying to play the hero wastes your precious resources and energy that you need for other tasks. Instead, be a hero for being able to survive in a wilderness setting with what you have and doing a very good job of it and being proud of the skills you have mastered.

Recognize and Accept Situations

When you find yourself in a rough or dangerous situation, learn to recognize the emergency, and to accept that it had happened. Acceptance is by no means that you like the situation you are in, or that you give up or are apathetic. It means you are thinking logically and not dwelling in a false reality of what you wish the situation really should be.

This allows you to think clearly and start finding solutions to get out of the situation by using all the means at your disposal. When you accept the situation you will have a focus and a goal to work towards your survival.

Adapt to Changes

Being able to adapt to situations as they change is a priority survival trait. Learn to roll with the changes instead of stubbornly refusing to accept that the situation or the environment has changed from what would be ideal for you. If you are on a wilderness trek and a storm comes up, accept that you need to find adequate shelter for the night. Being stubborn and trying to trek out through the storm is not being tenacious, it is being stubborn and foolish.

Find the best solution available for whatever your emergency situation is. Look for an alternative water source if your drinking water runs out, make a shelter or find an unoccupied cave to shelter in, and if something has happened to your food supply, start foraging. Stubbornness will result in you wasting your energy and the results could be bad. It is not easy to change your mindset from stubborn to adaptability, but it can be done with practice, and that is what survival is all about: adapt and thrive.

Avoid Unnecessary Risks

Learn to recognize the difference between a calculated risk and an unnecessary and foolish risk. In an emergency situation, you need to look at the risks you need to take and compare the rewards of the different risk options available. Weigh up each risk and then make an informed decision to the best option to take.

Grasping at straws and making uninformed decisions in haste is the recipe for disaster. This counts for wilderness and urban emergencies and the goal must always be to get out of a situation via the best option available with the minimum risk.

Conserve Your Energy

Living in the wilderness brings certain tasks that you would not normally have when at home. Needlessly wasting energy by not taking all available opportunities to make things easier on yourself will mean you have less energy for other tasks. Instead of erecting your own shelter, look around the area for natural caves, or any old building in the vicinity. Check out all these options and if any are viable, use them instead of spending time and energy putting up a shelter. This way you will have more time to rest and build up energy for the next task.

Get Creative and Improvise

Humans have been making things since the cavemen used rocks as implements. We still improvise in our normal lives when you need a tool and it is not handy. We are able to use the same creativity and improvise when we are out in the wilderness and an emergency crops up. The only thing that keeps us from improvising is our own fears. You may not want to look stupid or disappoint another person, or you have old fears from childhood. Whatever the reasons are, to survive in the wilderness you have to forget about everything and focus on improvising to create a solution to your present predicament. The goal is worth looking silly or improvising in ways that are totally outside the box—survival is worth everything.

Humor

This may seem like a strange trait you need for survival, but it can pull you through situations that seem quite desperate. While it is most inappropriate to laugh at sadness or start giggling at a funeral, ironic humor, often referred to as "gallows humor" is a valuable trait to help get you out of a nasty situation.

When the human mind is overwhelmed with stress the brain secretes more cortisol and less serotonin and dopamine which leads to depression and a feeling of hopelessness. Look at the situation ironically and find the ridiculousness and irony in the situation and make fun of it. Dark humor can help you or anyone in your group as they will focus on the ridiculousness of the situation and that clears the brain fog they are in.

Strong Work Ethic

These are words that apply to our daily lives, at work and at home. Some people learn early that their work ethic pays off in long term benefits. Others prefer to take any shortcut possible and skip doing tasks or chores they dislike and hope someone else will do it for them.

A wilderness trek is not taking off from work for a time and having a vacation in a mountain cabin with basic amenities. Reality will smack you hard if you are lazy and try to skip doing necessary tasks for your safety and health. If you have a lazy mindset, you need to practice changing this before you go on a survival trek.

Persistence, Resolve, and Endurance

Practicing your bushcraft skills, whether on a planned wilderness outing or in an emergency situation takes tenacity. Mental toughness and endurance have nothing to do with how tough you are physically, or how much stamina you have. It is about being able to persist in a situation where things are not going well or an unforeseen emergency occurs.

If you are in a group, keep checking each other to see how everyone is doing mentally. Prop up each other's weaknesses and lean on each other's strengths. Bonding gives everyone hope and understanding and heightens everyone's resolve to endure and get through whatever situation you all are facing.

Positive Attitude

Throughout history, humans have always had the will to survive, no matter how bad the situation might be. Our survival instinct is what brought us through wars, famine, natural disasters, and diseases.

So, how do you cultivate a positive attitude when you are stuck in a dangerous situation or an emergency? It is no use simply saying to a person that they must stay positive and not just give up. The best way to cultivate and maintain a positive attitude is to turn it around. Instead of taking a pessimistic look at your situation and focusing on what is wrong, make it an exercise in gratitude. Do a checklist of things you have to be grateful for in that bad situation.

Instead of thinking that you are stuck on a mountain in a storm, start listing the things that you have such as shelter, food to eat, wood for a fire to warm you, and first aid supplies to tend to any wounds you may have.

Pessimism literally sucks your strength and will from you, leaving you with no energy to do the necessary tasks to ensure survival, and it becomes a downward spiral.

Start a new habit in your life to find at least four or five things in your life to be grateful for. Practice this every day and at home and at work, wherever you find yourself. This is prep work for survival should you find yourself in such a situation.

Chapter 2:

Modern Tools for Primitive Living

Tools and our ability to use them is what sets humankind apart from the other animals on the planet. When cavemen invented tools for hunting it was a huge evolutionary step forward for us. Without tools, we would still live a precarious and primitive lifestyle.

Bushcraft and survival reconnect us to the way our ancestors lived, but with a big difference. We can use modern tools to live primitively in the wilderness. This is often a controversial statement as peo0ple have their own personal ideas about living in the wilderness. The purist survivalists feel that you need nothing more than a very good knife, and there is no need for other tools. This is fine for people who want to do it that way, but it is not the wisest decision to make for anyone who is a beginner in bushcraft.

When you start out on this journey of going back to your roots, it is always advised that you go as well prepared as possible. Learning survival skills should be enjoyable and make you eager to experience more and learn more. If you take on the wilderness without the right equipment, you are setting yourself up for failure. Once you have mastered all the necessary skills you can decide what tools you need and what you can do without.

So, where do you start, how do you know what you will need, and where do you find the necessary equipment for survival? We will go through the basics you need in this chapter to give you a good idea of what you need to start out with. The best place to start looking for the gear and tools you need is to go online. Search for bushcraft tools, survival gear, and wilderness equipment.

Explore all the online stores as this will give you the biggest variety in one place. Make sure that you read customer reviews on the products and then you can make informed decisions of what would suit you the best.

Clothes

A good rule to follow is fabrics that are natural, such as cotton and wool, are best. Synthetics are not the best option for the bush; it does not breathe and can be dangerous near campfires because of the chemical composition of the fabrics. A cotton and polyester blend is not a bad idea, as long as the ratio is 80% cotton and 20% polyester. Remember this is a guideline as each person has personal preferences as to fabrics and brands of clothing and you need to choose garments that you feel completely comfortable in.

Here we will deal with the basic list of clothing needed. You can add any extras as per your personal preference.

Gloves

Gloves are lightweight and easy to pack. It is always a good idea to have gloves in your backpack even in summer. Make sure you have at least one pair of glove liners (base layer gloves), a pair of waterproof outer gloves, and a pair of leather all-purpose gloves in your backpack. Gloves will save your hands when you climb up and over jagged rocks, moving branches from trees around, and save you from getting blisters.

Two Hats

Invest in two hats for any survival and bushcraft trips. A good woolen hat for warmth as you do not need to waste heat by going bareheaded. For the summer make sure you pack a sunhat as the sun can be very unkind. It will help to keep you cool and will protect your skin as well.

Hiking Boots

Personal preference and comfort must be your first consideration as your feet are your most precious asset in the wilderness. Always make sure that you pack at least one, but preferably two sets of spare laces for all trips.

Always look for hiking boots that fulfill the following criteria:

- Breathable material.
- Comfort is your top priority at all times. You cannot take on the wilderness in boots that will leave your feet blistered.
- Easy to maintain with minimum effort.
- It must give good ankle support.
- Lightweight enough to not put a drag on your steps.
- Made from waterproof fabric.
- The soles must be thick enough so that you do not feel sharp stones and rocky edges.

Pants for the Outdoors

The choice between shorts and long pants in summer comes down to what you personally prefer. Take note, though, that shorts will leave your legs exposed to scratches for bushes and thorns, as well as giving easy access to bugs that leave nasty bites and stings.

Criteria to look for in pants are:

- Pockets with zippers for keys, money, your wallet, etc. that you cannot afford to lose when on a trek.
- Cargo style pockets that are large enough to store some essentials that you need quick and easy access to.
- Comfort is non-negotiable. All your pants must be roomy and comfortable enough to allow you to move freely and be able to climb over obstacles with ease.

Socks

Socks and hiking boots go hand in hand in importance. You cannot walk in wet socks and need to prepare at all times to have the correct socks on hand. There are several options to consider:

- Regular socks, plus pack a few spare pairs of socks. Choose lightweight socks for summer and heavyweight socks for winter and cold climates.
- Invest in a few pairs of waterproof socks and pack them for trips. Waterproof socks consist of an interior knit sock, then a waterproof layer,

and an exterior knitted sock and are thicker than regular socks.

- Wool walking and hiking socks are long-lasting, very thick, and give extra comfort as these are padded.

T-Shirts

Polyester-cotton T-shirts are easy to wash and they dry quickly. Another option is polyester T-shirts, but the drawback of these is that they tend to cling to your body when you get wet or when you sweat.

Undergarments

Your regular underwear is fine for wilderness trips, as long as they are comfortable and do not constrict you. It is wise to invest in thermal base layer long sleeve tops and bottoms for winter or very cold climates.

Heavy Warm Outer Layer

You need a thick, warm outer layer for the intense cold when it is not raining. Always invest in a reputable brand and the best quality that you are able to buy. Always fit on the jackets to make sure it is roomy enough to go over whatever other layers of clothes you will be wearing under it.

Lightweight Warm Tops

The best option for lightweight, but very warm tops is fleece as it supplies the best warmth. Look for fleece tops that meet the following standards:

- Snug fit.
- High neck (polo neck) for extra warmth around the neck area.
- Has a neck zipper as this allows you to control the heat better.

Waterproof Garments

The weather can change very fast, so waterproof outer garments are essential to keep you dry and comfortable. You need a good waterproof outer layer that fits comfortably over your other clothes.

When you buy waterproof clothes you need to look for garments that will give you the following:

- Must have a hoodie, and look for one with a drawstring around the face if possible.
- It must not be overly insulated as you do not want it to be too warm and thick or it will make you sweat. The purpose of waterproof jackets and pants are to protect you from getting wet, not to supply extra warmth. Your other clothes provide the warmth that you need.

- The clothing you choose must be windproof as a chilly wind will drop your body temperature drastically.

- Look for clothing that is breathable with breathable sections inserted in strategic places that allow the garment to be breathable, but at the same time is still windproof.

- Make sure you buy a good brand that has a proven track record for durability and gives you the highest percentage of waterproof before moisture will start to soak through.

Essential Bushcraft Tools

There are several tools that are considered absolutely essential to have on hand for time spent in the wilderness.

The Sharp Edges

Knives are the most basic staple tool for any survival situation. No self-respecting outdoorsman would be caught dead without carrying at least one knife. A knife is the most versatile, multipurpose tool available to you. Ideally, your bug out bag should contain two knives.

Large Knife

A large knife should be your first choice if you had to choose only one.

Capabilities include:
- Clearing of vegetation.
- Digging.
- Cutting sticks and branches.
- Skinning and butchering game/fish.
- Self-defense against wild animals/humans.
- Preparing food.
- Cutting materials such as rope.
- Woodcraft.

Small Knife

Available as both folding and fixed blades, a small knife also offers great versatility.

Capabilities include:
- Preparing food.
- Skinning and butchering game/fish.
- Cutting vegetation and smaller branches.
- Whittling and carving.
- Self-defense.
- Shelter-building.
- Setting traps and snares.

- Phillips (flat head) screwdriver.
- Eating utensil.

Note: Beware thinking that a medium-sized knife can replace having a large and a small knife to save money and space. Medium knives are versatile and can perform many of the tasks the other knives can but it's not as efficient.

When investing in a bushcraft knife, there are several characteristics to consider.

Good blade and handle: Steel blades are the best option. Consider the strength of the steel, corrosion resistance, cost, and how well it retains its edge. Handles come in a variety of materials; investigate how well different materials handle wear and tear and ensure it fits your hand comfortably.

Size: Ensure that your knife fits comfortably in your hand and your bug out bag. Opt for a larger and a smaller knife instead of a single medium knife.

Weight: Consider the weight of your knife, as little as a few ounces more for a knife of the same size but constructed of different materials can become an annoyance after hours of carrying it.

Edge: Partially serrated blades offer slightly more versatility but are more difficult to sharpen.

Locking mechanism: If you choose a folding knife, it should easily fold away when you're not using it and remain open and fixed while you are.

Opening mechanism: If you opt for a folding knife, it should open quickly and easily.

Quality: A quality knife will stand the test of time and not break or otherwise become less effective aside from requiring blade sharpening.

Price: You don't need the most expensive knife on the market. Decide on a budget and invest in the best quality knife you can afford.

Brand: Brand is a personal choice and many outdoorsmen are loyal to their favorite brand. Research and choose a reputable manufacturer. Quality brands will offer quality products, which is something to keep in mind while deciding on the previously mentioned considerations.

Warranty: Choose a knife with an unconditional (aside from losing it) lifetime warranty. Such a warranty is also indicative of a quality knife from a good brand.

Ax/Hatchet

A multipurpose tool that is almost as versatile as a knife but not quite as capable of certain tasks.

They look similar but their differences will affect your choice. If you have space and can carry the weight, an ax is a better option for versatility.

So, what's the difference?

Ax	Hatchet
Bigger – requires more space	Smaller – requires less space
Heavier	Lighter
Used two-handed – more powerful strikes	Used single-handed – less powerful strikes
Bigger backswing – requires more space for use	Smaller backswing – requires less space for use
Uses: Felling or chopping down trees Splitting bigger chunks of wood Chopping up logs or bigger branches	Uses: Hammering or striking something Chopping down smaller trees or branches Splitting smaller chunks of wood

Ax/hatchet uses include:

- Clearing vegetation.
- Chopping wood.
- Shelter-building.
- Using the flat side to hammer or strike objects.
- Butchering bigger game animals.

Machete

A machete is a very large, curved blade that is primarily used for clearing vegetation but may also be used to cut materials and even butcher big game. If space is at a premium, a large knife can perform many of the same tasks.

Saw

Saws come in varying sizes and can be useful in building a shelter and sawing wood. Again, if space is at a premium, a large knife will suffice.

Blade Sharpener

Bladed tools are vitally important but blades dull over time, so the ability to sharpen blades is crucial.

Whetstone: A particular smooth stone that is wet with water before sharpening various non-serrated blades.

Requires skill to use but offers more versatility than knife sharpeners.

Knife Sharpener: Bought commercially, it's easy to use and suited for beginners.

Fire Starters

Being able to light a fire can be the difference between life and death in the wilderness, making fire starters essential.

Firestarters include:

- Matches and lighters (opt for butane lighters and water-resistant matches).
- Ferro rod.
- Flint and striker.
- Magnesium fire starters.
- Various natural means of starting a fire, some of which are detailed in chapter seven.

Water Filtration and Purification

Water is one of the most fundamental needs you must take care of in the great outdoors. Investing in a portable water filter and purification tablets are essential for your bug out bag. They come in different types and sizes. Choose a portable filter that suits your bug out bag and the space available. Water purification tablets will save you time if you can't boil the water and cool it first.

Fishing Line and Hooks

Being able to make even a rudimentary fishing device may be important if you find yourself in a survival situation. You can invest in a commercially bought, compact kit that is light and takes up little space.

Snare Wire

Snare wire works better than rope or cordage. It serves a single purpose and you won't have to waste precious rope if you find yourself in an emergency situation.

Compass

Having a compass with you is more reliable than a GPS as your battery could fail, leaving you stumbling around while trying to figure out the direction. Select a professional compass over a button compass if possible, as they are more accurate.

Map of the Area

Having a map of the area you are visiting is more than just a good idea. It's important to familiarize yourself with the area beforehand, but if you become lost, a map will help you determine the fastest route back to civilization by visually indicating nearby roads and highways, big and small towns and cities, water sources, etc. See more about the importance of maps and familiarizing yourself with the terrain in Chapter Eight.

Collapsible Bucket

A collapsible bucket is light-weight and space-saving, a useful tool for collecting water without contaminating your water bottle.

Tarp

Having a tarp in an emergency situation can be a life-saver. It is useful for hauling items, building a shelter, and even collecting rainwater.

Rope and Cordage

Paracord is extremely versatile in bushcraft and comes in a variety of forms from lengths of rope to paracord bracelets and lanyards which look cool and are easy to carry without taking up space in your backpack. Some uses of rope include:

- Traps and snares.
- Fishing.
- Shelter-building.
- Hanging wet clothes/blankets to dry.

- Hanging food out of reach of animals.
- Binding items together.

First Aid Kit

Whether you are simply driving your car on a regular day or heading out into the wilderness, you should never leave home without at least a basic first aid kit. You can buy a simple kit commercially which will be compact and have all the necessary basics in it. Remember to always carry a seven-day supply of any chronic or essential medication you may be taking in case of an emergency situation.

Bug Out Bag

In order to carry your bushcraft tools with you, you are going to need a good backpack. When choosing a backpack, consider the following:

Material: Choose a sturdy material that won't rip easily.

Construction: Look for quality stitching that won't come apart easily.

Attachments on the outside: Look for a variety of attachments that will allow you to carry additional gear on the outside of the backpack to save space on the inside.

Padding: Padding for shoulders, waist, or hip straps, and where it rests against your body is likely to increase comfort.

Ventilation: Mesh inserts in the backpack construction for ventilation will help prevent you from overheating in hotter conditions.

Water-resistant cover: Protecting your backpack from rain helps keep your gear dry and stops you from lugging around extra weight from wet material.

Compartments, pockets, and access: Compartments and pockets will help keep your gear organized. Ensure that all pockets and compartments are easily accessible from varying positions and angles.

Hydration Bladder: having a hydration bladder compartment saves more space than carrying water bottles and you won't have to take your pack off every time you want a drink.

Fit: Ensure that the backpack you choose fits well and doesn't put unpleasant pressure on your body or chafe.

Chapter 3:

The Power of Being Your Own Architect

Rope Craft

Rope craft is defined as the art of handling and using rope, which may include being able to make your own rope out of available materials around you. This is an important skill for any outdoorsman, survivalist, or bushcrafter to have as it is useful across the board when you are spending time in the wilderness.

Why is Rope Craft Important?

- Shelter-building.
- Raft-building.
- Rappelling down inclines.
- Carrying tools and supplies so that your hands remain free.

- Making a tripwire.
- Hanging food and supplies out of reach of animals.
- Hanging clothes out to dry.
- Fishing line or making a fishing net.
- Making a tourniquet to stem heavy bleeding. (Caution: Making and using your own tourniquet without the proper knowledge and skill can be just as dangerous as not stopping heavy bleeding.)
- Making a bola to catch animals or large birds.
- Making traps and snares.
- Rigging a makeshift pulley system.
- Tying items down in shelters or on rafts so that you don't lose them.
- Making primitive fire-starting tools.
- Making a belt that you can hook tools and supplies onto.
- Replacing broken shoelaces.
- Making a pet leash/collar.
- Making a rope ladder.
- Building a hammock.
- Making a human leash to link members in a group together and leaving your hands free.
- Making a splint or sling for injuries.
- Making repairs to supplies, shelters, etc.
- Tying sticks to the bottom of your shoes to create makeshift snowshoes.

- Brightly colored ropes can be used for signaling.

Tying Knots

Part of being able to properly use ropes in the outdoors is knowing how to tie sturdy knots that won't let you down by coming undone at the worst possible moment. Here are three basic but essential knots you need to know.

Square Knot

This knot is also known as a reef knot as it was used in centuries past by sailors for reefing their sails. This knot is not fool-proof but can be useful for quickly tying down non-essential items. Do not use this knot for joining pieces of rope together as it may come undone. It is important to make sure that both ends of the same rope end on the same side when you have finished tying this knot.

Bowline Knot

A bowline knot is an absolutely essential knot to know how to tie. It is used to create a secure loop at the end of a piece of rope. This knot will not jam and is easily tied and untied, unlike some other knots that may be easy enough to tie but become impossible to untie once they have been subject to tension.

You can create both small and large loops with this knot and the loops will be fixed, meaning that they won't be able to become smaller when subject to tension. It is a strong and reliable knot but because it is easy to untie once you've tied it, you should not rely on this knot in a critical or life and death situation.

You may have heard someone mumbling about a rabbit coming out of a hole, going around a tree, and then back into the hole while tying a knot. If you did, they were tying a bowline knot.

Double Sheet Bend Knot

This knot is also known as the Becket Bend knot and it is useful when you need to tie two ropes together, even if they are of different sizes or if they are made of completely different materials. Again, this knot should not be used in critical or life and death situations. It is important to make sure that both ends of the same rope end on the same side when you have finished tying the knot. The double sheet bend knot is more secure than the single sheet bend knot.

Basic Wilderness Shelters

When it comes to surviving in the wilderness, finding shelter is going to be one of your main priorities. As a rule of thumb, three hours is the average amount of time you can survive when you are exposed to extreme elements. Being out in the wild means that there are no hotels to check into so you're going to have to create your own and the sooner you start, the better your chances of making it through your survival situation.

Location is Key

Sure, you can build a shelter anywhere you like but that's not going to help you in the long run. The location you choose will determine your survival success and may end up making the steps for building your shelter easier. The first thing to consider is why you're building a shelter.

When you take up survival and bushcraft as a hobby, you are considering yourself an outdoorsman. This means that you place an emphasis on reconnecting with nature and not destroying it. If you are not in an emergency situation, choosing the right location will minimize the destruction necessary to construct your shelter. Nature is a sustainable resource if used wisely. If every outdoorsman went into the wilderness and started chopping down trees to build a shelter, we would quickly run out of trees. However, if you are in an emergency survival situation, doing a little bit of tree damage may be part and parcel of making it out alive.

Choose Your Spot

There are several factors to take into account when considering the best location for your shelter.

- Pre-existing shelters may be available and include caves, old buildings, and naturally occurring overhands.
- Take into account the local area's rules and regulations to prevent destroying threatened plant species or landowner disputes.
- Consider how long you will be using the shelter and adjust the size accordingly.
- Criteria for choosing a shelter location:
- There should be enough construction materials, such as wood and leaves, available without having to travel long distances to find them. Wood is an important resource for fire and shelter so there should be plenty of it.
- Don't build a shelter on or near animal paths, near insect nests, under rotting or dead branches, in the path of avalanches, landslides, or rock falls, or in a possible flood zone.
- Opt for an elevated area or a hill in case of rain and avoid low-lying areas such as valleys where temperatures drop at night.
- Be on the lookout for insects, spiders, and snakes on the ground and don't set up camp on

top of them or near their hiding spaces to avoid unfriendly encounters in your shelter.

- Look for naturally occurring level ground without having to flatten it out yourself.

- Look for good soil drainage so that your shelter won't flood if it rains.

- Look for a nearby usable water source but build your shelter at last 50 yards away. Don't build a shelter too close to rushing water as it will cover the sound of approaching animals or help calls.

- Look for the predominant wind direction and construct your shelter side-on with the opening facing away from the wind.

- Look for a safe spot to build a fire based on the weather, soil type, nearby plants that could catch alight, and available water to quickly extinguish a flame.

- Look for a spot where the available construction material will be suitable for the length of stay. If you are staying longer, choose a spot that offers robust materials that won't start breaking down while you're still using the shelter.

- If you are building a shelter as part of a bushcraft experience and would like others to join you, look for a spot that offers expansion possibilities with enough space and available construction materials.

Note: A good sport for constructing a shelter is at the edge of an open field near dense underbrush.

Building Materials for Shelters

If you are not in an emergency situation, you should opt for using naturally occurring building materials that don't require you to do damage to the environment.

Solid frame Shelters

- You don't have to use thick branches. Aside from the main supporting beams, smaller structures or shelters for shorter stays can be constructed out of sticks around as thick as your thumb.
- Choose straighter sticks instead of more crooked ones.
- Look for naturally Y-shaped branches and sticks for construction to conserve rope.
- Check for rot and possible insect nests within your construction materials.
- Remove protruding twigs or side branches from the main beams and sticks to prevent injuring yourself.

Materials for Roofing

Roofing materials refer to the additional materials used to insulate your shelter from the elements and you should view them similarly to roofing tiles. You will layer the materials over each other from the bottom upwards to help make your shelter waterproof.

Roofing materials may include:

- Dried hogweed logs
- Cane
- Long grass
- Ferns
- Spruce needle branches
- Leaves
- Moss
- Clay
- Survival cement (a mixture of clay, grass, and mud)
- Tree bark

Ground Cover

Tents have groundsheets that prevent the bottom of your tent from resting directly on the ground. This is important to insulate yourself from the cold that rises from the ground as it is this rising cold that will leech your body temperature more than the air temperature.

Similarly, you will need to use a layer of dry ground cover inside your shelter to insulate you from the ground. The materials used should be dry and not damp as dampness conducts cold.

Ground cover materials may include:

- Leaves
- Moss
- Pine needles
- Grass

Shelter-Building Tools

You may not have access to tools in an emergency survival situation. However, when practicing bushcraft as a hobby, there are a couple of tools you should always have handy for constructing a shelter.

- A sturdy survival knife for cutting and whittling sticks.
- A saw to cut branches.
- An axe for chopping or splitting branches or cutting notches.
- Rope or cordage to bind your shelter-building materials together.
- A shovel for collecting soil or sand.
- A tarp for collecting building materials and taking them back to your chosen location or to incorporate in the construction of your shelter.

Different Shelters for Different Needs

When you are deciding on what kind of shelter to build, there are a few things to take into consideration.

- The environment you are in will suit some types of shelters better than others including the predominant weather patterns and available building materials.

- The length of stay will have a hand in determining the type and size of the shelter you want to build.

- If you are in an emergency situation you will need to construct the simplest, fastest, and most suitable shelter for the elements and the materials you have available.

There are three main types of shelters that survivalists or outdoorsmen can make use of:

- Naturally occurring, pre-existing shelters such as overhangs, caves, old buildings, or hollowed-out dead trees (not rotting) are great places to start which will minimize the amount of effort you have to put into making your stay in the wild more comfortable.

- Emergency shelters are quick and easy to set up so that you can protect yourself from the elements in a survival situation without wasting time or energy.

- Semi-permanent shelters take more energy and time to set up than emergency shelters but they are worth the effort for a more comfortable stay when you aren't in an emergency.

Cocoon or Debris Shelter for Emergencies

This is the easiest and most basic form of shelter. All you need to do is gather up dry natural debris, such as pine needles and leaves, and build a mound of 24 to 36 inches in height and to a length that is a little bit longer than you are tall. Pack the material together well and then tunnel into the center of the mound, surrounding yourself with it like a cocoon. If you are in a pinch and need to find shelter quickly, this could be useful to bear in mind.

Tarp Shelters for Emergencies or Convenience

A tarp is an incredibly versatile material for anybody spending any length of time outdoors. It is particularly helpful when it comes to building shelters. A tarp is handy for building a make-shift shelter by itself. However, you can use it in conjunction with other building materials to fortify your shelter from the elements such as using it as a groundsheet or placing it under or over roofing material to improve waterproofing.

Shelters built solely of tarps aren't quite as stable or effective as other sturdier outdoor shelters but they are useful in a pinch and offer protection from the sun, wind, and rain. They can be constructed quickly and with little effort, making them an ideal quick-fix solution for emergency survival situations.

Tarp Wedge

This type of tarp shelter is best suited in windy conditions where the wind is coming predominantly from one direction. The aerodynamic wedge shape of this shelter offers better protection from wind and rain than other tarp shelters and is more secure because it has five (or more) tie-down points.

Lay a square piece tarp out flat on the ground with one of the four sides facing directly into the wind. Use stakes or other means to tie down both corners of that side of the tarp securely to the ground. Be sure not to tie down corners that are diagonally opposite to each other, they must be on the same side facing into the wind.

Once you have tied down the side of the tarp that is facing into the wind, move to the opposite side where both corners are still unsecured. Find the center of this side of the tarp and tie a rope or piece of cordage to the center.

Tie the other end of the rope to a sturdy tree branch and raise the center of the tarp until it forms a wedge shape.

When it comes to securing the remaining two corners, take the weather into consideration. When constructing this type of shelter in cooler weather, only raise the center of the tarp high enough so that the remaining two corners can still be secured firmly to the ground, offering better wind and rain protection. In warmer weather, raise the center so that the remaining two corners are lifted off the ground slightly before securing them to offer better ventilation.

Tarp Wedge A-Frame Shelter

This tarp shelter is similar to the tarp wedge shelter detailed above. You will need a few more natural supplies but it will be a little bit sturdier than a simple tarp wedge.

You are going to need to find three sturdy, straight branches. The longest branch should be longer than your tarp. If you are using a rectangular tarp, it should be longer than the shortest side of your tarp. The other two poles need to be no longer than your tarp.

Use rope or cordage to secure one end of the longest branch to a tree at about waist height. If you want to conserve rope, look for a tree that has a natural notch or branch that you can rest the branch in.

Lay the branch out from the tree at an angle facing into the wind and lay both shorter branches on the ground on either side of the longer branch so that they are positioned parallel to it. By laying the longest branch away from the tree into the wind, the opening of your shelter will be protected.

Drape your tarp over the branch so that there is an equal amount of the tarp on either side and tuck the excess tarp material around under the shorter branches. It should cover some of the floor of your shelter and the branches weigh it down where it meets the ground.

At the opening of your shelter, weigh the corners down some more, using rocks for instance, so that the opening stays stable and doesn't allow the shorter branches to move around.

Tarp Tent Shelter

A tarp tent shelter is easy to set up in next to no time. It can also be adapted for warmer or cooler weather, making it a versatile option in different climates.

Find two suspension points, such as two nearby trees, that are the height you want the top of you're a-frame shelter to be and tie rope or cordage between these two points.

Lay your tarp over this suspended rope so that it is even on both sides.

Secure the four corners of your tarp to the ground, pulling them slightly outward to form an A shape.

In cooler weather, secure the corners right against the ground. If the weather is warmer, give your shelter better ventilation by securing the corners slightly off the ground to allow a breeze to pass through underneath the edges.

Tarp with several eyelets along the sides can be further secured by adding more tie-down points, making your shelter a bit sturdier.

Tarp Wing Shelter

If you need protection from sun exposure or rain, a tarp wing can help you out. However, if you need shelter from the wind or cold temperatures, it isn't going to do you any good as it does not have any sides. A tarp wing shelter is simply a suspended piece of tarp acting as a 'roof.' If the breeze is warm and you want to make use of a tarp wing shelter, bear in mind that it will billow in even a small amount of wind which isn't conducive if you intend on getting any shut-eye underneath it.

Find four trees that are relatively close to each other in roughly the shape of a square and lay your tarp on the ground between them.

Use a rope to tie one corner of your tarp to the nearest tree. Decide on how high off the ground you want your tarp to be and then position the rope around the tree at that height.

Move to the corner diagonally opposite to the one you just secured to a tree and do the same with that corner, securing it to the tree closest to it at the same height as the other corner.

You will be left with two unsecured corners diagonally opposite each other. Secure these corners to the trees closest to them but secure them at a slightly lower height than the first two.

Tarp Burrito Shelter

If you need a quick and basic shelter in fair weather that requires no other building materials except just your tarp, then the tarp burrito shelter is just what you need. This is the most basic, no-frills type of tarp shelter but if the weather is really bad, you might want to consider something that offers a bit more protection.

Note: This shelter doesn't offer any ventilation and therefore you will experience a buildup of moisture on the inside produced from your body heat.

Lay your tarp out flat on the ground.

Take one side and fold it so that approximately 1/3 of the tarp is folded over on itself. Continue this process of folding it over until you reach the end of your tarp. Since you have folded it in thirds, the end result will be that your tarp is now 1/3 of its original width. Ensure that the tarp is folded over on top of the last flat end against the ground. The aim is that your bodyweight will hold the tarp down.

Now that you have a tarp tube, fold one of the open ends in under the tube to close it off. This will leave you with a tarp sleeve that is closed on all sides except the opening through which you are going to slide into it.

Note: You may need to adjust the amount you are folding over according to your body size, the size of the tarp, and whether you are adding a sleeping bag or not. The basic idea is that you want to fold the tarp over just enough to form a tube that you can slide into. You don't want the tube to be too wide so you may need to calculate how much you need to fold over to suit your needs. If you are using a sleeping bag, a good idea is to place the sleeping bag on the tarp before you start folding it over and simply rolling the tarp up around your sleeping bag.

Lean-To Tarp Shelter

A lean-to tarp shelter isn't going to offer shelter from harsh elements such as cold or wind. However, it can help keep you shaded, offer a small amount of wind protection, and may even ward off light rain.

This shelter is simple and quick to set up. Find two trees growing close to each other. Using the same side of your tarp, secure one of the two corners to each of the trees at your preferred height. Secure the two corners of the other side of your tarp to the ground at an angle away from the trees. If you intend to sleep under your lean-to tarp shelter, be sure to lay dry ground cover materials in a thick layer under the shelter.

Lean-To Shelters

A lean-to shelter is made by constructing a piece of shelter that can be leaned against another structure. You can use them between two nearby trees to offer limited shelter from sun exposure, wind, and maybe even light rain. For a lean-to shelter to offer a little more protection against the elements, lean it against a solid structure such as a fallen tree or a rock face which will provide extra shelter from the other side as well.

For a basic lean-to shelter, pick two trees that are close together and secure a long pole-like branch between them at an appropriate height. The size of your shelter will be determined by the height you secure that pole at. Your shelter should lean at about a 45° angle. The higher you secure the supporting pole, the larger the area of your shelter will be but that also means you will need longer 'stacking' sticks.

Once your supporting pole is securely in place, find and gather thinner sticks that are long enough to lean against that pole at a 45° angle from the ground and stack them against the supporting pole tightly together. The more gaps there are and the bigger they are, the less effective your shelter will be against the elements.

Once you have laid your stacking sticks against the support pole, use some brush to block up the remaining gaps. Once the gaps have been plugged, pack your lean-to shelter with other roofing material such as leaves and moss to improve the waterproofing and efficacy against the elements.

Note: When constructing a one-sided lean-to shelter between two trees, if there is a change in the wind or rain direction, your shelter will be rendered ineffective.

Semi-Permanent Shelters

While emergency shelters can come in handy as a quick-fix or if you find yourself in an emergency situation, they aren't suitable for longer stays or in more extreme weather. If you have the time and resources, setting up a semi-permanent shelter is the way to go. Aside from being more comfortable overall, they are more durable and offer you more protection from the elements.

A-Frame Shelters

The name says it all. The shape of this shelter is similar to an uppercase 'A.' These shelters are relatively quick and easy to construct depending on how much time and effort you really want to put into them although being more thorough will mean it will be more comfortable.

There are three main types of A-frame shelters:

- The classic or basic A-frame.
- The wedge A-frame.
- The tree-supported A-frame.

Basic/Classic A-Frame

This is the most typical version of an A-frame shelter but it does require you to put in more effort than the other two versions. The basic frame of this structure consists of five large branches or poles. The length and height of your shelter will help you calculate the length of these poles.

Find four sturdy branches or poles of the same length. Two poles will be used at either end of the shelter by creating an 'X' to support a central crossbeam. Find a fifth, longer pole that is the length you want your shelter to be and use this as the main crossbeam.

Tie the two shorter poles on one end of the structure together near the top using a shear lash. To do this, wrap the rope around the two branch poles a couple of times and then loop it through between the two poles a few times before tying it off. Make sure to lash the poles together far enough from the end so that the main beam can rest comfortably in the top part of the 'X.' Repeat this process with the other two shorter poles on the other end of the shelter.

Lay the central cross beam on the ground with one side facing the wind. This ensures that one side of your finished shelter will be facing into the wind to protect the openings at the ends.

At one end of the main beam, stand a pair of the supporting 'X' poles upright and space the bottom ends of these poles the width of your shelter base apart from each other. As you do this, they should cross near the top where you've lashed them together to form an 'X.'

Lift up that end of the main beam and place it into the top of the 'X.' Make sure that you leave enough overhang on the other side of the 'X' so that the beam won't slip out of position. You will now have one pair of upright support poles and the main beam at an angle from the top of those poles to the ground.

Repeat the process with the support poles on the other end of the main beam. Bring them upright, properly spaced apart at the bottom, and then lift the crossbeam into the top of the 'X.'

Note: For longer shelters, an additional pair of support poles may be needed in the center of the main beam to prevent sagging or collapse.

The next step is to gather up long sticks or thin branches that are the same length as the ones used to create your supporting 'X' poles. You will be laying these sticks along the sides of your A-frame shelter at the same angle as your 'X' poles so that they come to rest against the main beam at the top. Make sure that you stack them tightly together, leaving as few gaps as possible.

Once you have used sticks to create the sides of your shelter, it's time to gather up brush and moss to pack between the sticks and plug up any gaps. On top of that, pack a thick layer of grass, leaves, ferns, or other dry vegetation to improve insulation and waterproofing. Don't forget to cover the floor of your shelter with a thick layer of dried leaves and vegetation for ground insulation.

Basic or classic A-frame shelters are open at both ends. This means that they offer you shelter from the sun, rain, and wind but still allow airflow through the shelter. This means that any heat inside the shelter doesn't get trapped and kept inside. If you want to close off one of the two ends of your A-frame shelter, use another long supporting pole and prop it up against the 'X' supporting poles at the end you want to close off. Make sure it's leaning at the same angle as the rest of the shelter. Just as you did with the sticks on the sides of your shelter, stack sticks against the supporting poles in place, plug the holes with brush and moss and cover with a thick layer of dried vegetation.

Tree-Supported A-Frame

Building a tree-supported A-frame wilderness shelter is a little bit easier to do than building a classic A-frame shelter. If you can find one tree that has a natural Y-shaped crook in a branch or cup-shaped hollow, you can replace one set of supporting pairs of 'X' poles with the support offered by the tree. If you are lucky enough to find two trees growing close to each other with Y-shaped crooks or hollows, you are in luck because you can then suspend the main center beam between those two trees without having to create any supporting structures. Although the name says 'tree-supported' you can keep an eye out for almost any sturdy, naturally occuring support such as boulders and rocks, trees, fallen trees, etc. Any naturally occurring support that is sturdy enough to support the main beam and sides of your A-frame will work.

The same remaining general instructions for building the shelter apply as with the classic A-frame shelter.

Wedge A-Frame Shelter

A variation of the classic A-frame shelter, this one is slightly easier to build even though it's not the most efficient use of space. What it does have going for it is that it's sturdy, and takes less time and energy to build than its classic cousin. Instead of creating two 'X' shaped supports for both ends of this shelter, you will only be making one. The other end of the main beam will rest on the ground to create a wedge shape between the raised entrance and the back end of the shelter.

As with the classic A-frame, find two sturdy branches or poles to construct the supporting 'X.' Once you have lashed the poles together, stand them upright and rest one end of the main beam in the cradle. Leave the other end on the ground. Make sure that the end of the main beam that is on the ground faces into the wind for maximum wind protection.

Once your basic frame is in place, follow the same instructions as for the classic A-frame for stacking sticks against the side, filling in the gaps, and adding layers of vegetation for insulation and waterproofing.

Unlike the classic A-frame which is more comfortable, this variation of the A-frame structure is designed to offer shelter to sit in and sleep in. It should be kept short, only about one and a half times your body length.

Quinzhee Snow Shelters

Where there's snow there's the opportunity to build a snow shelter. If you're not in an emergency situation, these can be a lot of fun to create. One of the easiest snow shelters to build is a quinzhee.

Snow Shelter Dangers

As much fun as a snow shelter may be to build, they come with some risks to be aware of.

Any shelter, when not constructed properly, can collapse on you. However, when it comes to a snow shelter collapsing, it poses the threat of burying you in the snow. Collapse can happen for a variety of reasons. Someone, or even an animal, standing on the shelter can cause it to cave in. The snow melting over time can weaken the structure and cause it to collapse. Another reason for a snow shelter caving in is because of inadequate sintering.

What is sintering and how does it affect your snow shelter? Sintering is the change in a snowflake's structure because of slight melting or because the snow has been put under pressure. Sintering can happen because heat is transferred to the snow when you touch it with your hands or by compacting it. If adequate sintering doesn't take place, the snow may not stick together well enough to maintain its shape and collapse.

Before you go out and try to build a snow shelter on your own, it's a good idea to thoroughly research how to pick the right snow and get some practice in with someone who knows how to build snow shelters. This will help you to develop the skill and knowledge necessary to guard against collapse.

Snow shelters often require a lot of work and effort to build which leads to sweating. You are also likely to get snow on your clothes which will melt. This combination will result in damp clothing which quickly matches the ambient temperature of your environment and can cause hypothermia. If you are going to be building a snow shelter, a set of dry clothes to change into will be necessary so that you can stay warm and dry.

Quinzhee Shelter Design

Unlike an igloo, which is made of compacted blocks of snow, a quinzhee is constructed by creating a mound of snow and compacting it so that it forms a solid heap of snow. Once the mound of snow has been sufficiently compacted, you can begin hollowing out a cavern on the inside.

You will begin by piling snow to create a mound and compacting it as you acquire more and more snow.

Once you have built up a large pile of compacted snow, you are going to need to gather up sticks that measure more than 12 inches in length. Push these sticks into the snow all over the mound to a depth of 12 inches. They will later guide you as to how much to hollow the inside of the quinzhee out so that the walls aren't too thin in places.

Allow your mound of snow to sinter for at least 90 minutes but a period of two hours is preferable. Remember that sintering is a vital part of preventing collapse so it's best not to rush the process.

Once you have left your snow to settle, begin digging into the mound and hollowing out the center to create a room. This is best done with something like a shovel as your hands will become very cold after a while of digging.

If you have a tarp handy it can be used to pile dug-out snow onto the quinzhee and to drag out of the quinzhee. It can also be used to lay down on the ground like a groundsheet for the floor of your snow shelter on top of which vegetation can be packed to form a layer of insulation.

As you dig out the inside of the shelter, be mindful of the sticks you pushed into the snow, and don't dig out any more snow once you reach the ends of the sticks.

Quinzhee Tips

- Once the interior has been dug out, you can smooth out the inner walls. Smoothing the inner walls is important as it will help melting snow or condensation run down the walls instead of dripping onto you.

- Dig a little trench all the way around the inner edge of your quinzhee so that any water that runs off the walls will pool in the trench.

- Build an elevated sleeping area to keep you off the floor and out of any potentially pooling water.

- Warm air rises while cold air sinks to the lowest point. This will result in a colder temperature on the floor of the quinzhee where you will be sleeping. Dig a tunnel somewhere near the side of your quinzhee at the bottom. Dig it out at an angle which will offer cold air somewhere to pool lower than your sleeping area.

A properly built quinzhee can offer you a few nights of shelter but remember not to use one quinzhee for too long before you either move on or build another one as the risk of collapse increases over time.

Chapter 4:

Get Your Game On

Outdoorsmen, bushcrafters, survivalists—anyone who embraces the outdoors and being able to live off the land—take pride in the ability to find food naturally through foraging, fishing, and hunting. If you are in an emergency situation, being able to find food is incredibly important as it drastically increases your chances of survival until you are either rescued or manage to make your way back to civilization. You can survive for three weeks without food but starvation isn't fun and you will start feeling the effects of going hungry within hours of your last meal.

Hunting

There is a wide variety to choose from when it comes to hunting methods. You can choose modern rifles, a common traditional method, or you can choose something a little more historic such as traps and snares. Each outdoorsman has their preferred hunting tools. Many hunters who are in it for the big game prefer rifles as you don't have to get too close to a large animal to bring it down. However, others enjoy using bows and arrows, slings, throwing spears, or even the primitive hunting method of using blowguns. All of these hunting tools have one thing in common: they require skill in order to use them successfully. If you don't have much, or any, hunting experience or find yourself in an emergency situation where you don't have hunting tools available, your best bet is to use traps and snares. Setting and using basic traps and snares takes little to no skill or experience, all you need to know is what you're hunting and the animal's behavioral patterns.

The Importance of a Good Knife

Every bushcrafter, hunter, survivalist, or outdoor enthusiast will agree wholeheartedly on at least one thing: a good knife is essential. Your knife is going to be one of your most versatile and useful outdoor tools. A good all-around knife will serve you well in various aspects of being in the wilderness from building a shelter and hunting to self-defense. Let's focus on finding food. With a good knife you are able to:

- Dig up edible tubers and the roots of plants.
- Cut up edible plants.
- Create traps and snares or even basic spears.
- Kill prey (not every animal caught in a trap or snare will be dead by the time you check on the snare and in this case, you will need to kill it yourself).

- Skin, gut, and cut up prey.

As you can see, every aspect of acquiring food is made possible and easier when you have a good knife and that's before you even get to cooking it.

Weapon Considerations

It doesn't matter what weapon you are using when hunting, you need to give it some consideration.

Rifles give you only one shot to bring down your prey as the shot will scare off the animal you're hunting as well as any other animals in the area.

A bow and arrow is a quieter hunting weapon but requires a lot of skill and closer proximity to the animal than a rifle.

Spears are quiet but you need the skill to throw them and to wield them so that you sufficiently injure the animal so that it cannot escape. Using a spear also means you have to get a lot closer to your prey which puts you at risk of injury or even being killed by a larger animal. Having to get closer to your prey also requires you to be very observant, very quiet, and very agile with fast reactions. If you are not silent and don't mask your scent, your prey won't come anywhere near you. If you're not fast enough then you'll end up spearing nothing but thin air.

Traps and snares are very basic and easy to use; you can set one and leave it alone for several hours before checking on it. The only thing traps and snares require is that you know what animal you are hunting, its habits, how to track its movement, and where to put the trap or snare so that it is effective.

Consider Your Prey

Not only do you need to give your hunting weapon consideration, but you also need to think about what prey you will be hunting. Some animals are easier and less dangerous to hunt than others. Whenever the topic of hunting is brought up, the most common image that comes to mind is deer or big game hunting. Bringing down large game might seem enticing but if you're just one person spending time outdoors, or you find yourself in an emergency situation, large game isn't the best option. Big game might provide you with more meat than smaller prey but most of that meat will quickly spoil without refrigeration.

So, what are the easier smaller prey animals to hunt?

- Squirrels
- Rabbits or hares
- Foxes
- Birds

If there are small deer in the area, they might be a good option as well but bear in mind that if an animal is too large for you to eat within a day or so, the meat will go to waste.

Another aspect to consider about your prey is your hunting technique. While it's entirely possible, you're not likely to use a rifle for fishing. Nor are you about to go around making noise or chasing your prey if you're hunting alone. Those may be obvious examples to the point of being somewhat ridiculous but the concept is sound. Different prey and habitats require different hunting techniques. Your hunting technique may also change based on whether you are alone or in a group and whether you have hunting animals, such as dogs, with you. Hunting as an individual requires you to be silent and extremely observant. It is also often a patience game when slowly stalking your prey without giving yourself away or lying in wait hidden from view and waiting for your prey to come along without noticing you. Hunting with dogs or as a group offers you the opportunity to flush the animals out into an area where it is more easily taken down.

Note: If you are not in a survival situation, you need to know the local hunting laws, hunting seasons, and the presence of threatened or endangered animal species.

Consider Your Skills

If you find yourself in an emergency survival situation, you have no choice but to hunt, fish, or forage for food in order to sustain yourself. However, if you are venturing into hunting as part of embracing an outdoor lifestyle, you need to consider the skills it takes to be able to successfully pull off a hunt.

Before you can even consider hunting, you need to develop a sound knowledge of the terrain and available prey animals as well as how to track them. Knowing the environment and lay of the land will help you predict where you will find prey animals, where they may bed down, and where to look for them if they are wounded during the hunt and you need to pursue them. Different animals have specific areas within the environment that they will prefer or frequent. Some common spaces may include open fields, dense underbrush, water sources, etc. Different animals will also have different routines and active times of the day. Knowing your prey will help you determine the best times of the day to hunt it. Once you know where to find the animal and what time of the day to go on the hunt, you must be able to track it. It doesn't help to wander around blindly, hoping to stumble upon an animal. If you cannot track your prey, you cannot determine the usual paths and where to lie in wait or choose the best spots for traps and snares. It's a good idea to scout your hunting area before your hunt, take photographs of the tracks you find, and identify them with a tracking guide so that you know which animals frequent which paths.

The Importance of Primitive Hunting Techniques

Human beings have been hunting for as long as they have been around but the methods and techniques used for modern-day hunting differ greatly from those used in primitive times. Cutting edge technology provides us with so many advanced gadgets and hunting tools that it is no longer about the hunt to survive, it is about the hunt for sport.

As high-tech and comparatively easy as hunting has become today, all of these advances are not foolproof. When you are dropped into an emergency survival situation, you may either not have those gadgets with you or they may fail. What you will be left with is whatever you can scrape together from your environment. This makes the knowledge of creating and using primitive hunting techniques a crucial part of outdoor survival.

You can check back to Chapter 2 for some ideas on primitive survival weapons and how to make them.

Note: Primitive hunting techniques such as using spears or a bow and arrows require a lot of practice to learn the skills necessary to be able to successfully hunt using these tools.

Hunting Tips

- Plan your hunt in advance, scout the area, determine the game you can hunt, prepare your weapons according to prey and habitat, and pack your supplies well so that you have everything that you need, including emergency supplies and a first-aid kit.

- Make sure that you wear enough blaze orange or "hunter's orange" so that you are visible and recognizable to other hunters.

- Tell friends and family where you are going and what you are doing so that they can inform authorities of where to look for you if anything goes wrong.

- Learn how to skin, gut, and cut up your game meat so that you don't waste spoiled meat through contamination or incorrect handling practices.

- Understand your game and its handling requirements. Mild weather will spoil meat faster than colder weather. Birds should be skinned or plucked and dressed as soon as possible. Small game like squirrels and rabbits must be skinned before they go stiff, etc.

- Enter your hunting area well ahead of your hunt. This way any wildlife you disturb has time to settle down before you start your hunt.

Remember, your game isn't just on the lookout for you; they are taking their cues from the other wildlife around them. Your scent will also have time to dissipate, which is another tell-tale sign animals pick up on when you've been in the area.

- Park your vehicle a distance from your hunting area and enter the area as quietly as possible to avoid disturbing wildlife or alerting your prey to your arrival.

- Make frequent stops to take stock of your surroundings and pick up on signs of prey activity such as tracks and droppings. Hunting is a patience game, you may end up sitting still for hours waiting for your prey to show up and all the while you need to remain observant.

- Keep wind conditions in mind when hunting. Strong winds make detecting predators more difficult for prey animals and therefore they may be inclined to remain hidden in thick brush. The direction of the wind is also important as being downwind from an animal will carry your scent on the breeze which will spook the animals.

- Aim for the kill and not just to wound. Hunt efficiently, quickly, and painlessly wherever possible by voiding a fast-moving animal or one that is too far away.

- During a hunt, anything can go wrong. If your prey ends up wounded and not killed, you must be prepared to track it and kill it irrespective of how far it continues to run after you've wounded it.

Tracking

The art of tracking animals is as old as the human race itself. It is a learned skill, passed down through generations, that helps to teach people about the environment they find themselves in. Have you ever come across an animal track on the ground and wondered what it belonged to, what it was doing, where it was going, how long ago the track was made, and where the animal is now?

That is something that happens regularly because the art of effective tracking is rare in our modern world. Many people can recognize an animal track as belonging to an animal and they know that it means the animal was there but they can't gather much else from it.

What is Animal Tracking?

Tracking animals is the ability or skill to collect the evidence of local animals through their foot tracks, their droppings, and other signs of their presence and then to use that evidence to gain insight into the animal's behavior and eventually find them. Effective tracking employs specific knowledge and techniques that help the tracker to identify the animal tracks and signs of their presence to figure out how fast they were traveling, the direction, what their behavior is, and even tell the likely sex and size of the animal. Not only does this skill help an outdoorsman to locate and hunt prey, but it also allows them to determine whether there are any potential threats in the area.

The foundation of tracking depends on having an in-depth understanding of nature and not only how but also why everything is intricately connected to each other. You must have a goal to gain a true and full understanding of the workings of nature as an ecological system which includes all the elements from big game and predators down to plants and insects, as well as nature's energy cycles as they relate to the passage of time and within space. It is this deep understanding of nature that allows effective trackers not only to follow an animal but to get closer to it through anticipating its behavior within the environment. It takes time to learn this skill. When you first encounter an effective tracker, it can seem as though they possess some magical power that allows them to read so much into what looks perfectly unimportant to you. However, once you gain that understanding, nobody can take it away from you and it will serve you well as a survival skill.

Tracks vs. Signs

Animal tracks typically refer to the imprint of an animal's foot in the ground. However, it can also refer to imprints made by other parts of their body such as head, tail, antlers, or any part of their body that touches a surface and leaves an imprint. When you study the shape, pattern, size, and other distinguishing characteristics of an animal track, you can determine what animal left the track and even what it was doing when the track was made.

Animal signs refer to any other evidence, aside from tracks, that indicates an animal was present. This may include worn out traveling paths, droppings, bits of fur or skin, animal markings on plants or trees, food scraps, broken plants, and more.

Why is Tracking Important?

Not only will tracking help you during a hunt, but it will also alert you to dangerous situations such as when predators are present. Predators not only pose a risk to the game, but they also post a serious threat to you as well. It is important to be able to identify the tracks and signs of predators in the area so that you can remain aware of their presence and pick up any clues about their behavior. Tracking is also useful in situations where you want to find water or find your way somewhere. Understanding animal behavior and being able to identify tracks can help you navigate your way through a wilderness area and you don't just have to track animals. Being able to identify and follow signs of human passage through the area may help you find your way out of a wilderness area if you get lost.

Characteristics of Reading Tracks

There are several universal principles for reading tracks of both wild and domesticated animals which will help you begin to learn how to read tracks:

- The presence of claw impressions. Some animals, like cats, have retractable claws but many others, like dogs, do not. When an animal does not have retractable claws, there will be claw impressions at the ends of the toes.

- The shape. The shape of a track can help you identify the animal even if the track is slightly worn away. For instance, cat tracks are circular while dog tracks are more oval. Observing the shape of a track can help you identify the animal even if worn away tracks look similar to the untrained eye.

- Negative space. In most tracks, you will find what is called negative space. If you look at the track of a dog or cat, you will see an imprint of the toe pads and heel pad made in the ground. The spaces where the dirt was not imprinted on between the toes and the heel pad is called negative space. If you look at the impression of a horse's hoof, you will see an imprint or the outer part of the hoof but the middle will be left raised. That middle space is the negative space.

- The size of the different parts of the track. When looking at cat tracks, you will notice that the heel pad is larger than the toes. When looking at dog tracks, you will notice that the toes take up more space in the track than the heel pad. Being able to observe the size ratios of the different parts of a track can help you identify the type of animal it came from.

- The number of parts of a track. Different animals will have different numbers of toes, for instance. Identifying how many distinguishable parts a track has will help you identify the type of animal it came from.

- Stride length and track size. Not only the size of the track but the length of space between the front and back feet tracks of an animal will give you an indication of its size.

- Gait pattern. The pattern that several tracks make can tell you what type of movement the animal was making. A walking pattern indicates a relaxed animal while a running pattern indicates a nervous or excited animal that is either running away from danger or towards something like a mate.

- Impression depth. A tell-tale sign of a more urgent type of movement is how deep the impression is. A relaxed animal that is simply strolling along will leave shallower impressions than a running animal that is exerting a lot more downward force when taking each step.

- The age of tracks. Fresh tracks and old tracks will give you an idea of how recently the animal was in the area. If you are using tracking for hunting, it's important to learn how tracks age and how to tell approximately when they were made. It's not going to help your hunt if you are following two-day-old tracks.

- Track direction. The direction the toes or front of the foot are facing will tell you which direction the animal you are tracking was moving in.

- Animal signs. There will be times when tracks are not visible but other signs of animals are. Knowing what to look for and where will help you pick up on signs that different animals have been in the area. Some signs to look for are scrapes on trees, fur stuck in tree bark, rocks, or bushes, droppings, and signs of feeding. All of these signs will give you clues as to what the animal was, what it was doing there, and what direction it went in even before you pick up the tracks.

Tracking Signs That Are Not Tracks

When it comes to tracking an animal there are many different signs that can indicate its presence in the area even if you don't see their tracks.

Runs and trails are worn into the environment through frequent use leading to feeding areas, water sources, bedding areas, or shelter. Trails may be used by a wide variety of species while runs are typically only used by a few animals or a single species. Trails are typically worn right down to the dirt and display many different tracks. Runs are better for setting traps than trails.

Bedding areas may be used only once or frequently, often in a thicket or thick brush, and can be recognized as a depression in the plant life.

Feeding areas are seasonal and specific to a particular species. They include grass fields, open areas in a forest, berry patches, or other areas where nutritious vegetation can be found. Research what different prey animals eat so that you can be on the lookout for those specific feeding areas when tracking or hunting. Some feeding areas will display signs of grazing when you take a closer look at the vegetation which could indicate recent feeding activity.

Animals will scrape their antlers or claws on harder surfaces like trees. They will also rub themselves up against surfaces to scratch and itch or mark territory. Be vigilant and look for scratch-and-rub evidence to determine whether there are animals in the area.

Fur and feathers will indicate an animal's presence in the area. Hair and feathers can snag on branches, trees, or get stuck in places the animal rubs itself against. They can also be found in bedding areas or at sites of a recent kill.

Droppings are another dead giveaway that an animal has been in the area. Fresh droppings will tell you that the animal may not be far off. Some animals also use droppings to mark their territory. Researching the local game will help you know when an animal marks territory with droppings. When you come across those droppings, you will have an indication that you are in an animal's territory.

Seeing Tracks in More Detail

When tracking, it's important to glean as much as you can from an animal's track in order to track them effectively. Here's how you can get the most out of seeing a track in as much detail as possible.

Use the sun to your advantage by viewing the track from an angle that doesn't place it in your shadow or any other shadow if possible. Viewing the track in proper light will help bring out the detail. If it is dark, use a flashlight. If there is some shade you cannot avoid, use a mirror or something shiny to reflect light onto the print.

View the track from a variety of angles and different heights. Stand up, crouch down, get down really low on your hands and knees. The more angles from which you view a track will allow you to see more detail.

Be patient when tracking; don't go barging through the wilderness. Take it slowly and be careful not to trample vital evidence that may be around the track.

Study not only the track but the area around it as well for other clues.

Make a sketch of the track as best you can and make notes about other details you observe.

Do Your Research

Before going into any wilderness area, you should research the area and the local wildlife in that area. Print out or buy a guide on the local animals and their tracks. Doing your homework will help you gain an advantage when you are tracking, especially if you are doing so as part of hunting. When you start out as a beginner tracker, it's important to have references on hand so that you can learn to identify tracks as you go along.

Trapping

For the inexperienced hunter or anyone who finds themselves in a life or death emergency survival situation, trapping is one of the easier ways to procure meat for food. It's never foolproof but it's your best chance if you aren't skilled at other forms of primitive hunting techniques such as using spears.

Trapping: Advantages and Disadvantages

- Trapping is a passive form of hunting, requiring little energy to build the trap and check on it. This helps you conserve energy if you're in a dire situation.
- There are some basic traps that even novices can build and set to use for hunting.
- Some basic traps can be made from just some wire or cordage and materials found around you.
- Unless you are in an emergency survival situation, some local laws prohibit the use of trapping. You must check the laws governing the wilderness area you are going to visit.

- Traps and snares can be indiscriminate, they don't differentiate between young and old, too small or the right size, prey animal or predator. Traps and snares that work will catch anything that ventures into them whether it was intended for that specific species or not, putting the lives of threatened or vulnerable species at risk.

- Some animals may be able to free themselves from traps if they are not set or constructed correctly.

- If an animal gets free from a trap or snare, it may be grievously wounded.

- Prey caught in a trap or snare may be snatched up by a natural predator, rendering your efforts fruitless.

- Traps and snares require patience; you have to wait for your food to come to your trap.

- You may have to set multiple traps to achieve success. The more traps you set the more chances you have of catching something legal and edible. The downside is that you also increase the risk of catching and injuring or killing something that isn't edible or is endangered.

Types of Traps

Traps come in many forms, sometimes they are specific to a certain species or type of animal, other times they can be used on a variety of different animals. When you are out in the wilderness and find yourself in an emergency situation, trapping or snaring small game is your best bet for success. Let's take a look at some basic and relatively easy traps and snares that even novice survivalists can create and use.

Note: Traps and snares are frowned upon in the general recreational outdoors and bushcraft community. This is because, unlike hunting with other tools, you cannot really target a specific species or specific age, weight, gender, or health of an animal. They do not offer you the ability to make an informed decision regarding the animal you are catching. Traps and snares should only be used in emergency survival situations when you don't possess the tools or skills to use other hunting methods.

For traps and snares to be more effective, they should be set on obvious game paths. Try to identify the game you are targeting and look for species-specific runs for that animal. Avoid setting traps and snares on general animal trails that are frequented by a wide variety of species. In order to set traps and snares, you will need to have knowledge of and experience with tying a variety of stable knots to prevent your prey from breaking free and escaping.

You need to check your traps and snares regularly to see whether you have managed to snare prey and that they are still properly set. Checking frequently also ensures that if you do manage to catch prey in your snare or trap, a predator won't walk off with your meal. Setting traps and snares within earshot of your shelter will allow you to hear when an animal has been caught.

Apache Foothold Trap

This trap was originally intended to snag big game like deer. However, it may be useful for catching medium-sized prey.

- Find a suitable animal path on which you can identify the tracks of your intended prey.
- Dig a hole into the ground to a depth of approximately 20 inches. This depth is suitable for both medium and large prey. The hole doesn't have to be wide, it just has to be deep enough to trap a variety of game animals of differing leg-length and size.
- As you dig, your hole may become filled with groundwater. This isn't a problem. Dig to the appropriate depth and the water will further serve to camouflage your trap.
- Once you have dug the hole, find sticks of 12 inches or longer and sharpen the tips to create stakes.

- Insert six of the stakes in a circle into the sides of the hole, approximately halfway between the bottom and the top. Leave a gap in the center of the stakes through which the animal's foot can fit.
- Insert the remaining six stakes in a circle into the sides of the hole near the top. You should now have two rings of stakes protruding from the sides of the hole with a gap in the middle for the animal's foot.

What the stakes will do is trap the animal's foot for a short period of time. This allows the snare to tighten around the animal's foot while it is struggling to get free. The animal will most likely free its foot from the hole but in the struggle the snare should have tightened around its foot, further trapping it.

This snare requires strong rope or wire that can withstand the jerking force the animal will exert while trying to get free. A wire is a better choice than rope as it is less likely to present the animal with an opportunity to free itself.

- To create the snare, create a loop at one end of the rope or wire and feed the other end through that loop. You will now have a large loop that can sinch closed.

- Lay the looped snare over the top of the stakes, leaving sufficient space for the animal's foot to pass through as it falls into the trap.
- Secure the free end of your rope or wire around a suitable, healthy tree that will withstand the force of a struggling animal.
- The length of your snare rope or the wire leading to the tree should be sufficient to allow the animal to move around a small amount but not allow it too much space to roam.
- Finally, camouflage your trap by covering it with leaves and other vegetation debris as well as covering the snare rope or wire that is secured to the tree. It's not necessary to bury the trap and snare wire, you only need to loosely cover it so that it isn't obvious.

Basic Snare

The importance of knowing how to construct and use a basic snare is that it is applicable across a wide variety of game from small prey such as rabbits or hares to larger game like deer. This snare is as simple as they come and all you really need to do is tie a snare loop, secure the other end, and hang it in place.

Tie a snare noose with rope, cordage, or wire. The wire will hold its shape much better than rope and increase your chances of success. To tie the noose, create a loop at one end of the rope or wire and feed the other end through that loop. You now have a noose that will sinch closed.

How big your noose needs to be and where you should place it depends entirely on your intended prey. Decide on the game you are trying to hunt, find a run with their tracks, and consider their height. For instance, when snaring rabbits, the noose should be hung low to the ground and be made only large enough that their head and ears fit through but not the rest of their body. Try to find parts of the run where there are overhanging branches and side foliage that will both support and disguise your snare. Place your snare at a height that is approximately where the animal's head would be while walking.

Secure the free end of your snare to a healthy, sturdy branch or tree that can withstand the force of the struggling animal you intend to catch. If you are catching a rabbit, a good branch should do the trick. If you are trying to catch a deer, you need to have a strong tree trunk to secure the snare.

Note: Wire snares hold their shape well. Rope or cordage snares require you to use the surrounding vegetation to prop them open until the prey animal walks into them.

Pitfall Trap

Unless you want to spend two days digging a pit, this trap is best suited for smaller prey animals.

- Dig a hole into the ground that is deep enough for your intended prey to be unable to jump or climb back out.

- Make the entrance to the hole narrower and the bottom larger. It may be worth smoothing out the sides or walls of your trap to make it more difficult for your prey to climb back out.

- Loosely cover your trap with debris. You can also create a raised cover over the debris out of rocks or tree bark to entice small prey to use the area underneath as a hiding spot at which time they will fall into the trap.

Note: When you check the trap, be sure to remove any prey with care as a trapped animal, regardless of how small they may be, will react aggressively.

Where to Set Traps and Snares

As discussed in the previous tracking section, the best place to set up traps and snares is on an animal run. If you are able to identify a run and follow it, set your trap near the end or the beginning. At points of entry and exit of a run, animals will be focused on avoiding any possible threats and may not be as tuned in to their surroundings as when they are more relaxed. This gives your trap a better chance of going unnoticed. Make sure to camouflage the trap and set it in a position where the animal won't simply sidestep and pass it without being caught.

Decommission Traps and Snares

It is crucially important that all traps and snares set during your time in the wilderness are decommissioned and discarded before you leave the area or return home. This will prevent animals from becoming entrapped or ensnared unintentionally which would cause unnecessary injury, suffering, or death.

Caution

Traps and snares are a firm favorite of indiscriminate poachers. They are therefore dangerous to out of season, threatened, or vulnerable prey. For this reason, many areas prohibit the use of traps and snares. It is important to check the local laws governing the wilderness area you will be in to ensure that you are not unintentionally setting traps and snares where it is illegal to do so. It is different if you are in a life and death situation but if you are spending time outdoors recreationally it could cause you a lot of legal problems.

Fishing

When spending time outdoors, whether for pleasure or in a survival situation, you are going to need to find a source of drinkable water. However, that's not where the value of bodies of water such as rivers, streams, and lakes ends. They may also provide you with a source of food. Learning how to fish with the bare necessities on hand is both a vital skill and also a fun experience when you have the time to experiment recreationally.

Simple bushcraft fishing kits that provide a basic hook and some fishing line are always a good idea to have on hand, but you can also learn how to craft your own fishing supplies if you don't happen to have a kit with you.

Note: If you are completely new to fishing, experimenting with basic handmade bushcraft fishing methods can be a fun way to spend time outdoors or with friends and family. If you are serious about learning to fish recreationally, it's worth putting in the time and effort to discover what style of fishing you are interested in, learning about the technique and equipment, and what fish you are likely going to be fishing for.

Making Your Own Fishing Hooks

You're not always going to have a fishing book handy, especially if you're in a survival situation, and sometimes while fishing you'll end up forfeiting your hook to a fish. When you're out of hooks, you may not be as out of luck as you think. There are several items that you may already have with you or are able to source from the natural environment that will help you catch a fish.

If you happen to have a safety pin handy, you can employ it as a makeshift fishing hook. Open the safety pin. Straighten it out so that the arm with the pointed tip creates a straight line with the arm that has the head on it. Bend a section of the arm with the pointed tip so that it resembles a hook and tie your fishing line to the head of the safety pin.

If you don't have a safety pin, you can fashion a hook out of a stick. The size of the stick will depend on the size of the fish you intend to catch. Use a stick that is approximately 1/3 the thickness of your index finger. For larger fish, the stick should be as long as your ring finger. For medium-sized fish, the stick should be as long as your pinky finger. Strip the stick of its bark, sharpen both ends to points, and cut a groove around the center of the stick. Secure your line in the groove. When baiting this stick hook, hold the hook and the line parallel to each other while baiting. Bait it in such a way that the bait will temporarily hold the hook and line together. Once you have baited your hook, hold the line straight up; the fishing line and stick hook should be vertical and not have the hook hanging horizontally perpendicular to the line. They need to be facing the same direction so that the fish swallows the hook and some of the line together. The bait should hold them together until the fish swallows the baited hook. Once the bait and hook are swallowed, the bait should loosen and the hook should get stuck in the fish's throat.

Making Your Own Fishing Line

If you don't have an actual fishing line handy, you can always improvise. You can use a piece of paracord by removing the inner strands to use for the fishing line. You can also use dental floss if you have some with you. If neither of those is available, you can use an animal's intestinal lining gathered from a recent successful hunt.

Making Your Own Fishing Rod

You can easily fish by holding your fishing line in your hand. This is known as hand-lining. This can also be done by wrapping your line around a small piece of a branch which may be easier on your hands if you happen to snag a feisty fish. However, you can also fashion a natural fishing rod for yourself. Ideally, you need to find a thin, flexible branch, such as a newly growing branch or a branch from a young tree. An inflexible stick will also work but having some flex in your 'rod' will help tire a fighting fish out. Once you have found a suitable flexible branch, strip the bark from the outside. Cut a groove around the end you are going to tie your line to, and then secure your line in that groove. The groove will help keep your line from slipping off the end.

Finding Bait

You can cast your line and hook into the water and wait but you're going to be very hungry by the time you catch anything if you actually do manage to catch something. To entice a fish to swallow your hook, you are going to need bait. Recreational fishermen will be able to give you a lecture on the value of knowing exactly what kind of bait is best for what kind of fish. This is great knowledge to have, as fish who prey on insects aren't going to give berries a second look. This is where you have to have patience. If you are uncertain of what the fish you are trying to catch normally feed on, you're going to have to figure it out by trial and error. If you start off with meatier bait items and find that the fish just aren't biting, you may need to try baiting your hook with something else, like berries.

Some common bait ideas include:
- Insects
- Worms and grubs
- Frogs and toads
- Snails and slugs

- Lizards
- Animal and other fish guts

If you're really stuck for bait, you can try to attract fish to bite by baiting your hook with a small piece of brightly colored material or a shiny button.

Spearfishing

Spearfishing is not quite as simple as casting a line into the water with a baited hook on the end and waiting for a fish to come along and bite. However, it is useful for fishing in shallow water or if you want to try your luck at pitting your wits against the fish. This can be a fun activity to share with friends and family when spending time outdoors together.

Making a Spear

- Find a thick stick; look for the straightest possible stick you can find. Ensure that it is approximately eight feet in length.
- Use your knife to split one end of the stick down the middle. The split shouldn't be too short or too long but will vary according to the size of the fish you are hunting. When aiming for medium-sized fish, make the split about six inches long.

- Wedge the split open with a small piece of stick at the base of the split so that your spear has two prongs.

- You can make your spear a little sturdier and minimize the risk of breakage or the split getting bigger by wrapping and securing a piece of rope or cordage around the spear. Wrap the rope from the base of the split toward the prongs until you have wrapped it to just above the piece of stick wedged in the split.

- Sharpen the end of each prong to a point. If you want to harden the tips, you can fire-harden them by placing your spear prongs over a fire.

Using a Fishing Spear

- Use your dominant hand to hold the spear and place your other hand further up the shaft to use as guidance. When you thrust your spear forward, the driving power should come from your dominant hand.

- Slowly lower the prongs of your spear into the water. Having your spear already in the water will improve your aim by reducing the amount of light refraction that occurs as light hits the water.

- Very slowly move your spear closer to the fish until the prongs are only a few inches away.

- Make sure to hold your spear so that the prongs are at a 90° angle to the fish. This will give you a better chance at success as if one prong misses, the other should pierce the fish.
- Use a quick jabbing motion for your strike and don't retract the spear immediately. Strike and hold the fish in place once it has been pierced so that you can reach into the water to take it out without it slipping away when you lift your spear.
- If you have pierced a fish in the gut with your spear, you must clean it, gut it, and rinse the inside of the fish out thoroughly as soon as possible to prevent contamination.

Cooking Meat and Fish

Yes, meat and fish are consumed raw in various dishes in many countries but it's not a good idea when you're out in the wild. Many prey animals carry parasites and bacteria that can make you very ill and can only be killed through cooking the meat. Always cook any meat or fish found taken from the wild.

Remove the guts. Organ meat is enjoyed the world over and is even sometimes seen as a delicacy. However, when you're hunting and fishing for food in the wilderness it can be very dangerous. All guts should be removed unless you are a professional outdoorsman with years of experience and you know what you are doing. It's better to be safe than sorry and stick with muscle meat and leave the organs out of your meal.

Many people enjoy their meat to be cooked medium-rare or even rare when they are dining out or at home. If you're out in the wilderness, you are going to have to make a compromise and cook your meat well. Overcooking your meat may make it tougher and change the flavor slightly but it is better than becoming ill in the wilderness. Wild animals carry different bacteria and parasites to domesticated animals in the meat industry and only by cooking the meat thoroughly will you avoid becoming ill or even dying from those parasites or bacteria.

Always discard any waste from hunting and fishing far from your campsite. If possible, bury the waste but always remove any edible waste from your campsite and dispose of it as far away as you can to avoid attracting predators and scavengers, some of whom you don't want to come face to face with.

Preparing Game for Cooking

- Never make a kill or skin and gut your kill near your campsite or where you store food. This attracts wild animals.

- Slit the throat or remove the head and hang the animal upside down to allow the blood to drain.
- Skinning is easier once the animal carcass has had time to cool.
- When skinning your game, don't press or squeeze the belly. Doing so could cause urine to contaminate the meat.
- If the animal has musk glands, remove them.
- When removing the guts, pinch the bladder closed to prevent urine contaminating the meat.
- Various internal organs are edible but if the liver is spotted or mottled, discard them all.
- If you are keeping the liver to cook, remove the gallbladder.
- When cutting up your kill, cut along the grain of the meat.

Note: If you have never skinned and gutted an animal before, it's a good idea to learn how to do it before going on your first hunt so that you don't risk contaminating the meat in any way.

Preparing Fish for Cooking

Before you can cook your fish, you need to prepare it. Don't clean and gut fish near your campsite or where you store your food as it will attract wild animals.

- To remove fish scams, rub the back of your knife blade against the fish from tail to head so that you are rubbing against the grain of the scales. Thoroughly remove all the scales as they are not edible.

- You can cook fish with its skin on so skinning isn't necessary.

- Be sure to use a very sharp knife to gut the fish and try not to puncture any of the internal organs. Slice along the belly, remove all guts, and rinse the fish out thoroughly.

Chapter 5:

Forage for Food and Medicine

One of the oldest arts our ancestors have passed down from generation to generation is foraging for food. Today nobody has to forage for their meals, all you have to do is walk into a local supermarket and pick something off the shelf. However, if you are going to be spending time outdoors it can be a fun activity and it can also save your life if you find yourself fighting for survival in an emergency situation. Learning which plants are edible and which can be used for medicinal purposes takes time. It's not something that you can dive into headfirst for risk of poisoning yourself, or worse. Many species of plants look similar to each other and while one may be edible, the other could kill you. To make matters more complicated, there are plants that have both edible and toxic parts and you would need to know which part is which. Further, still there are plants that have parts that are only safe to eat once they have been cooked while others can be eaten raw. As you can see, it's a skill to identify plants and requires an intimate knowledge of your natural environment.

However, it is a skill that can be learned and a knowledge base that can be built up over time.

Tips for Learning to Forage

- Buy a good book. A good book that explains the characteristics of edible plants and has illustrations to depict what they look like is a good place to start building up your knowledge base.
- Find a mentor. Even with book knowledge, learning to forage successfully takes hands-on experience. Find someone who has experience and knowledge to forage with so that you can hone your skills with their help to avoid accidental poisoning.
- Keep a foraging journal. Documenting the plants you come across will help you commit the knowledge to memory. The act of writing down details by hand helps you retain information better. Try sketching the plant if you can, it will help you focus on observing the finer details and commit the appearance of the plant to memory better.
- Learn the habitat of the different plants in your local and surrounding areas. Not all plants grow in the same environment. For instance, those

found at lower altitudes won't be found at higher altitudes and those found in wooded areas won't be found in open grassland areas.

- Learn which plants grow alongside each other. It is common for different species to grow near each other. Finding one means that the others are usually not far away.

- Discover seasonal plants. Berries, for instance, grow at certain times of the year. Knowing growing seasons will help you keep an eye out for different plants and have a better idea of what might be edible based on knowing what is in season and what is not.

- Learn about edible and poisonous plants in your local and surrounding areas. You don't necessarily have to go far from home to find either. Starting locally will build up knowledge of your immediate surroundings and you can then begin to move further afield and expand on that knowledge.

- Learn which parts of plants are edible and which aren't, which must be cooked to be edible and which can be eaten raw, and which plants have both edible and toxic parts.

- Don't just learn the common names of plants. Many species of plants share a common name and while some might be edible, others may not. Classifying plants according to their Latin names is much better as you can identify plants for sale as safe or unsafe by simply asking.

Tips for Actively Foraging

- To begin with, forage as a group of friends. As they say, "Safety in numbers." This doesn't just refer to foraging accidents that could happen in the wild. You are able to make more informed decisions about plants by drawing on their knowledge.
- If in doubt, leave it out. This is a cardinal rule for foraging. If you are not 100% sure that the plant you are looking at is safely edible, don't forage it.
- Forage sustainably. Nature is a renewable resource but if everyone suddenly goes out foraging and takes more than they need or more than a respectable amount, it's not going to be as renewable or sustainable. Respect nature and your fellow foragers by not taking too much or more than you can eat before it goes off.
- Only pick the part of the plant you intend to consume. If you only need the leaves of a plant, for instance, pick sensibly. Don't pull up the whole plant and don't pick all of the leaves off a

single plant, both of which would kill the whole plant.

- Don't forage protected or vulnerable plants in the wild. Just because they occur abundantly in your area doesn't mean that they are as abundant throughout the habitat they grow in. Your local area might be only one area of abundance while the plant is scarce throughout the rest of its range. Picking these plants in your area because they appear to be abundant will decrease the overall number of plants in the habitat range.

- If you intend on foraging wild plants for regular use, consider growing them in your own garden so that you don't have to remove wild resources. Again, it comes down to respecting our ever-decreasing wild natural areas by investing in sustainability.

- Never pick plants that appear to be less than 100% healthy. Check whether the plant is discolored, wilted, has decaying parts, spotting, etc. Even if the illness appears to be in a single part of the plant, it's better to skip it altogether and look for a healthy one. A plant illness may affect the edibility of other parts.

- If you are foraging wild water plants, check that the water they are growing in is not contaminated as contaminated water may make an edible plant unsafe for consumption.

- Don't forage in unsafe areas which include areas that have been sprayed with pesticides or near busy roads. Hazardous chemicals in these areas settle in the soil and can affect new plants for a long time to come.

- Even if you know a plant is edible, if you have never eaten it before, exercise caution when including it in your diet. Changes in diet and the introduction of new foods can temporarily cause your body to have an adverse reaction such as an upset stomach until you get used to it. There is also the possibility of an allergic reaction. It's best to try a small amount first and see what happens before eating any more.

Getting Started

When you start out foraging for edible plants, begin with common edibles in your local area. Don't start trying to find any and all edibles at once. Familiarize yourself with the most common varieties first and slowly expand from there.

Some common edibles include:

- Amaranth - the *amaranthus retroflexus* species and others.
- Asparagus - *Asparagus officinalis.*
- Burdock - *Arctium lappa.*
- Cattail - *Typha.*
- Clovers - *Trifolium.*
- Chicory - *Cichorium intybus.*
- Chickweed - *Stellaria media.*
- Curled Dock - *Rumex crispus.*
- Dandelion - *Taraxacum officinale.*
- Field Pennycress - *Thlaspi vulgaris.*
- Fireweed - *Epilobium angustifolium.*
- Green Seaweed - *Ulva lactuca.*
- Kelp - *Alaria esculenta.*
- Plantain - *Plantago.*
- Prickly Pear Cactus - *Opuntia.*
- Purslane - *Portulaca oleracea.*
- Sheep Sorrel - *Rumex acetosella.*
- White Mustard - *Sinapis alba.*
- Wood Sorrel - *Oxalis.*

Some signs that you should avoid a plant include:

- Fine hairs, spines, thorns.
- A soapy or bitter taste.
- Sap that is discolored or milky.
- Beans, seeds, or bulbs in pods.
- Plants with foliage resembling that of carrot, parsley, dill, or parsnip.

- If the grain heads have black, pink, or purple spurs.
- A growth pattern consisting of three leaves.
- If the woody parts of the plant and leaves smell of almond.

When a plant displays one or more of these characteristics, it may be toxic. That is not a hard and fast rule as some edible plants will display these characteristics but it gives you a guideline if you are unsure.

Medicinal Plants

Not all plants foraged are superbly for food value. Some of them have medicinal properties and have been used for centuries to help humans treat certain ailments. This is useful information when spending time outdoors as you can turn to natural remedies to help treat some health issues you may pick up during your time in the wilderness or in an emergency situation.

Some examples of medicinal plants include:
- Willow Bark – *Salix* may be steeped into a tea that can be used to treat swelling, fever, aches, and pains.
- Fennel - *Foeniculum vulgare* can be steeped into a tea to treat bloating, stomach upset, and nausea.

- Yarrow - *Achillea millefolium* leaves and flowers may be used to treat coughs, fevers, and to help the blood to clot which slows down bleeding.
- Dandelion - *Taraxacum officinale* can be made into a balm to help treat joint and muscle pain.
- Plantain – *Plantago* can be made into a poultice for its anti-inflammatory properties.
- Comfrey - *Symphytum* can be made into a poultice or a compress for healing wounds and aiding in the healing of fractured bones.
- Cleavers - *Galium aparine* aid in removing congestion from the body such as cholesterol deposits, mineral deposits in the urinary tract and liver, and congestion in the lymphatic system.
- Joe Pye weed - *Eutrochium purpureum* may help treat gout, kidney stones, gallstones, and arthritis.
- Goldenrod - *Solidago spp.* helps treat kidney stones, urinary tract infections, incontinence, stomach upset, diarrhea, fever, and congestion associated with the common cold or the flu.
- Violets - *Viola spp.* can be made into a nourishing lip balm.

Universal Edibility Test

The universal edibility test can help you determine whether a plant is safe to eat or not but it is not foolproof. However, it can be useful to know the procedure and follow it if you happen to be in an emergency survival situation if you are in dire straits.

- Identify and separate the different parts that make up the plant (roots, stems, leaves, buds, flowers, fruit). You are doing this as you need to test each part of a plant individually to see whether that particular part is edible. Remember, not all parts of all plants are edible. Some plants have both edible and poisonous parts in the same plant.

- Pay attention to the smell of each part of the plant. If it has a pungent, unpleasant smell then it's probably not safe to eat.

- Take each part of the plant that you are testing and place a small piece on the inside of your wrist or elbow. Do this individually and wait a few minutes. Pay attention to any skin reactions such as itching, burning, stinging, numbness, or any other negative reactions such as a rash forming. An adverse reaction to skin contact with that part of the plant indicates that it is not safe to ingest.

- If no negative contact reaction presents itself, cook a small piece of each piece of the plant that is safe when it makes contact with your skin.

- Once cooked, don't just eat the plant. The next test it to see if there is a contact reaction when the cooked plant is placed on your lips. Wait roughly 15 minutes to see if any negative reactions occur such as those indicated above for the skin reaction test.

- If no reaction occurs on your lips, take a small bite of the plant part and chew it. Hold the chewed bite in your mouth for 15 minutes and see if there is a negative reaction on the inside of your mouth.

- If the plant part has a soapy or bitter taste, spit it out immediately and don't wait for an adverse reaction.

- If there are no reactions on the inside of your mouth after waiting for 15 minutes, you can swallow that bite or spit it out and take another small bite to swallow. This time you must wait several hours so that the plant can work its way through your digestive system to see if there is any negative reaction such as nausea, stomach upset, etc.

- If there is no negative reaction to the small bite of the ingested plant part, you can assume that it is safe to eat.

Be aware that there are wild plants so toxic that even the tiniest ingested bite can cause serious illness or even death. If you are in doubt, refer to the characteristics listed above that could possibly indicate a toxic plant.

Note: It is important that the process of the universal edibility test be repeated for each individual part of the plant. Again, just because one part is edible doesn't mean the others are and if you simply assume that you can eat the whole thing because one part proved edible, you could suffer grave consequences.

Chapter 6:

Water, the Source of Life

While a human being can survive three days without water, you will certainly start feeling the effects of dehydration long before then, especially in an emergency survival situation. Not only does dehydration start to wear down your physical capabilities, but it also starts to affect your cognitive ability. Basically, without sufficient water intake, your brain starts to suffer. Among other side effects, dehydration can cause dizziness and headaches, even delirium. Even if you are just spending time outdoors recreationally, this can severely impact your health and mental status.

This is even more important when it comes to an emergency situation. When your cognitive capabilities suffer in a survival situation, your chances of making it out alive severely decline by the hour. This is why you have a limited amount of time to locate a safely drinkable source of water as soon as some more pressing survival needs, such as shelter from the elements, are taken care of. Even if you can identify a drinkable source of water, you still need to have the time to purify it further before you drink it, making it one of your top priorities, so important that you should build your shelter nearby a good source of water.

Why Is Water So Important?

Approximately 60% of your body is made up of water. Water is necessary to keep your body functioning as a cohesive unit. How much you need will vary based on several factors such as your activity level, whether you are healthy or sick, even the kind of climate you live in can affect how much water you need to drink to stay healthy.

Water is used to keep all your body's cells, tissues, and organs functioning. It does this by keeping them moist. Think about how uncomfortable it is when you have dry eyes. Water helps keep them lubricated. Lubrication is necessary to keep your joints moving and your spinal cord protected.

The liquid part of your blood, known as your blood plasma, is 90% water. Without sufficient water, your blood thickens and is made more concentrated. This may create an electrolyte and mineral imbalance which will affect muscle function. Because your heart is a muscle, an imbalance of electrolytes affects the performance of your cardiovascular system. On top of all of this, when your blood becomes more concentrated, the amount decreases, and this and your blood pressure drops, causing dizziness.

Because water is vital for organ function, dehydration affects your brain. Your brain consists of 75% water. When your body becomes dehydrated, it affects your mental ability such as your ability to pay attention and remember things. When your blood isn't able to conduct electrolytes properly to your brain, it causes confusion and a kind of foggy-headed feeling.

Water is part of your digestion process as it aids in breaking down food and the absorption of nutrients from that food into the bloodstream. The soluble fiber in food becomes like a gel when water is present and this slows the process of digestion down. When digestion happens at a slower rate, your body is able to absorb a sufficient amount of nutrients instead of simply passing through and out the other side.

Water is a vital part of eliminating waste from your body. It does this by allowing you to urinate, sweat, and defecate. Your kidneys remove waste from your body through urination. It helps to prevent solid waste from piling up by keeping your stools moving and soft. It's not a cure for constipation but it does contribute to preventing it along with fiber.

Your body can better regulate its temperature if you have enough water in your system. It does this by allowing you to sweat, which, as it evaporates off your skin, helps to cool your external temperature down. When your external temperature cools down, so does your core temperature.

Signs of Dehydration

- Thirst.
- Dizziness or feeling light-headed.
- Fatigue.
- Infrequent urination.
- Dark yellow urine with a strong odor.
- Dry mouth, eyes, or lips.

There are common symptoms of dehydration and there are lesser-known signs that may often be overlooked in milder dehydration. These are not hard and fast indicators but may be possible signs.

- Bad breath.
- Sugar cravings.
- Headaches.
- Flushed or dry skin.
- Fever and chills.
- Muscle cramps.

Severity of Dehydration

- Five percent body fluid loss: thirst, nausea, irritability, weakness, cognitive impairment may set in after only two percent loss.
- 10% body fluid loss: headaches, dizziness, possibly even speech impairment, vision

impairment, physical movement impairment, and more serious cognitive impairment.

- 15% body fluid loss: severe hydration sets in and the symptoms are intense, vision and hearing impairment, severe cognitive impairment, fatigue, light-headedness, difficulty moving, painful and very infrequent urination, and even delirium.

- When you lose more than 15% of your body fluid, death becomes a very real risk.

Dehydration in a survival situation can severely impact your chance of surviving. When your ability to think clearly becomes impaired, you are at risk of making bad decisions and not being able to draw on any knowledge that could help save your life.

Conserving Body Fluids

On average you lose between two and three liters (67–101 fluid ounces) of your body's water daily. The majority of the water you lose is through breathing. Every time you breathe out, you are breathing out moisture as part of that breath. Sweating is another body function that speeds up water loss. Even spending the whole day resting in shade, you will have a loss of about one liter (33 fluid ounces). When you are in a wilderness survival situation, conserving body fluid is vital.

- Rest in the shade.
- Only perform tasks necessary for survival.
- Perform tasks at night when it's cooler.
- Eat only as much as you need to survive as digestion causes water loss.
- Eat carbohydrates as they require less water to digest than protein and fats.
- Don't drink alcohol or smoke cigarettes as your kidneys increase water loss to detox your body.
- Breathe through your nose as mouth breathing increases water loss.

Finding Water and Collecting It

Water can be found in various, sometimes surprising, places in the wilderness.

Collecting water may be made much easier through the use of a collapsible bucket which is lightweight, easy to carry, and takes up less space. You won't have to use your water bottle to collect water which would leave trace amounts of unfiltered water in the bottle. You don't have to drink a lot of unfiltered water to become ill from bacteria, all it may take is one drop. A collapsible bucket for water collection will also help you stir up less mud by skimming water off the top, extending the life of your water filter as it doesn't have to filter out unnecessary debris.

Low lying areas, like valleys, collect water as gravity pulls it from the highest point toward the lowest. Identify sources of water from a higher altitude by looking for lusher, greener patches of plants.

Another obvious source of water is rain. Collecting rain for drinking can be done using some sort of container or even a tarp.

Dew occurs in areas with hot days and cold nights and can be collected by laying a tarp out on the ground. Dew will form overnight which can be poured into a container. Hanging a piece of clothing up overnight will collect moisture from the air and can be wrung out into a container. Wrapping a piece of clothing around your legs if you walk through dewy vegetation will collect dew from the plants it comes into contact with.

Groundwater may be found at sites near water sources that appear to have dried up. Digging into the ground a few feet from a water source that doesn't look completely clear may provide you with water that has been filtered through the ground which is kind of like a natural water filter. Boil groundwater before consumption. Groundwater holes should be one to two feet deep, water will pool into the hole and can be a good source for a longer-term stay.

Water collects in natural 'containers' such as rock crevices and tree crotches.

Plants can be a good source of water. As plants 'breathe' they give off moisture. Wrap living, healthy leaves on a branch in a plastic bag, and wait. The plastic bag will collect the moisture given off by the leaves. Tie the plastic bag at an angle with the top being higher than the bottom.

You can find water in large trees with thick trunks by tapping it at an area just above a large root. Cut a slice into the tree, about an inch thick at an upward angle to allow the moisture to drip downward. You can use a large leaf or big blade of grass wedged into the slice, facing in a downward angle, to allow the water to drip into a container. Tapping trees also offer a source of tiny amounts of minerals and sugars.

Trees to tap include, but are not limited to:

- Birch.
- Maple.
- Boxelder.
- Palm.
- Walnut.
- Poplar.
- Sycamore.
- Hickory.
- Hackberry.
- Elm.

Don't tap evergreen trees as the sap can be too thick to offer adequate hydration. If you cut into a tree and a milky or darkly colored sap is produced, try a different species of tree as it may be unsafe for consumption.

Snow can be melted by boiling it which will also purify it. Don't swallow it whole as this will lower your core temperature which is dangerous in cold conditions. You can also melt snow by collecting it in a container and putting it in your pocket.

Water Safety

When you find a water source, it doesn't automatically mean that you can drink that water. There are water sources that could cause illness or even death if you consume the water.

There are five common types of water contaminants:

- Turbidity refers to invisible particles in the water that make it appear unclean.
- Parasites refer to single or multicellular organisms that live inside a host, often causing illness. An example of parasites is parasitic worms.
- Bacteria are single and multicellular organisms that may cause illness but don't need a host to survive. An example of an illness-causing bacteria is E.coli.
- Viruses are even smaller than bacteria and while they don't need a host to survive, they do need

a host to be able to multiply. An example of a disease-causing virus is Hepatitis A.

- Chemicals can pollute water and make it undrinkable such as pesticides that may run off into natural water sources from nearby farmland.

Another type of water to be aware of that should never be consumed is stagnant water. Because it's not moving, it's the perfect breeding ground for contaminants like bacteria, viruses, and parasites.

Aside from turbidity, most of the other contaminants aren't visible to the naked eye. Water may appear to be clean but that may not necessarily be the case. If you come across water that appears clean and clear, look for signs of life.

- Are there plants growing at the edges?
- Are there animal tracks leading to the source of water?
- Are there insects or even algae on or in the water?

Almost all forms of life need water to survive. If there aren't any signs of life, the water probably isn't safe to drink.

Finding the cleanest water possible is actually quite easy. Running water is often your best bet and once you find it, travel upstream to the source where the water is likely to be the cleanest. Groundwater is another source of drinkable water, the ground acts like a filtration system that generally filters out a lot of unwanted contaminants. Finally, the least reliable source of clean drinking water is rain, however, you can't necessarily just wait for it to rain.

Making Water Potable

Even if a source of water seems clean, you should never just start drinking it. Aside from chemical contamination, there are ways and means to get rid of the other possible contaminants.

There are four ways to make water drinkable.

- Distillation is the process of heating and then cooling water as a means of purifying it.
- Filtration is the process of passing water through a filter in order to remove particles.
- Boiling water reaches temperatures that kill the organisms that may be present.
- Chemical treatments use chemicals to kill organisms that may be present in the water.

Solar Stills

A solar still can be used when you can't find an obvious water source. It's a slow process and doesn't deliver a lot of drinkable water but it can be useful. The sun's heat evaporates water from the soil which condenses into a liquid when it comes in contact with a cooler surface.

- Locate an area where the sun will shine on the ground for most of the day and dig a hole approximately three feet wide and two feet in depth.

- Dig a small hole in the middle of the hole you've just dug out so that you can rest your water container in it.

- Lay the plastic sheeting over the hole and secure it with rocks. Don't stretch it too taut as you need the center to dip slightly downward.

- Place a rock on the center of the plastic sheeting, directly over your container. It should create a cone shape pointing down. Allow it to dip enough so that as the water vapor condenses into liquid, the water can run down the plastic toward the center and drip into the container but don't allow it to plug the container. If the plastic plugs the container, the water will run down the outside of the container and back into the soil.

Fire Stills

A fire still works faster than a solar still. The steam from boiling water is captured and condensed to produce clean drinking water.

- Boil water in an airtight container with a tube leading out of it. The steam will condense in the tube and run out of the tube into a collection container.
- Cover a pot of boiling water at an angle so that as the steam condenses on the cover it will drip toward the downward slope of the cover and into a collection container.
- Create a tripod over a boiling pot of water using sticks and hang an absorbent material over the pot so that it absorbs the moisture as the steam condenses into water when it comes in contact with the cloth. The cloth can then be wrung out into a container.

Water Filters

Dirty water can be filtered to produce cleaner water which can then be purified with chemical treatment or by boiling it.

There are various commercial portable filters that are light, easy to carry, and don't take up much space.

However, if you find yourself without a filter, you can make a bushcraft filter.

You can make your own filter out of various naturally occurring items such as sand, gravel, and charcoal leftover from wood burned for a fire. The trick is to filter the water through various layers starting from coarse at the top to fine at the bottom. There don't have to be many layers as it is the fine layers that are the most important, especially the charcoal layer.

Cut the bottom off of a plastic bottle and remove the cap.

Turn the bottle upside down and place a layer of fabric at the bottom and then a layer of fine charcoal on top of that.

On top of the charcoal create several other layers in the following order:

- Dirt.
- Sand.
- Grass.
- Gravel.

Pour the dirty water through the filter. The coarser layers will begin filtering out larger debris and as the water passes through finer and finer layers more and more debris will be filtered out.

Boiling Water

It is imperative that water be boiled or treated with a chemical purifier before you drink it. Filtration may help to remove debris, and ultrafiltration may help catch some pathogens but it's not 100% effective. You can bring filtered water to a rolling boil (around 100° Celsius or 212° Fahrenheit) and boil it for at least one minute at altitudes lower than 5,000 feet (1,000 meters) or at least three minutes at altitudes above 5,000 feet. This will kill off any pathogens in the water but will not remove chemical contamination.

Chemical Purification

Bleach is a common method for purifying water. Ensure that it has no added cleaning chemicals or scents and that it is not color-safe. To use bleach as a purifier, add 1/8 teaspoon (0.625 ml) to one gallon (approximately 3.8 liters) of water. It is very important not to add more bleach than that amount as higher concentrations are harmful.

A two percent iodine tincture can be used to purify water by adding five drops of the tincture to one liter of water. Add 10 drops to a liter of water if the water is cloudy. Allow the water to stand for a minimum of 30 minutes. It is important not to add more than this amount as iodine in higher concentrations could be harmful.

Diluted hydrogen peroxide of three percent to 10 percent strength can be used to treat water. Add 1/8 cup (approximately 30 ml) of the dilution to one gallon of water. Hydrogen peroxide for purifying water is not approved by the U.S. Environmental Protection Agency.

Commercial water purifying crystals are available. Simply follow the manufacturer's instructions on how to use them. This is a very handy option for purifying water in the wilderness as they are compact, light, and easy to carry.

Tablets and crystals: There are different types of water purification tablets and crystals, all of which are designed to simply be dropped into the water. Iodine and potassium permanganate can come in tablet or crystal form. Sodium chlorite (a form of chlorine) comes in tablet form.

Chapter 7:

The Story of a Spindle and

a Board

One of the most basic and important survival skills is being able to light a fire in a variety of different weather conditions. If you find yourself in a dire emergency situation your ability to survive drops to next to nothing if you cannot light a fire because of its many uses such as warding off hypothermia and allowing you to boil water to purify it.

Not All Wood is Equal

You may think wood, is wood, is wood, right? Not quite. Different wood has different properties when it's burned. Some wood burns brighter, which is great when you need light. Some wood produces hot coals that burn for a long time, which is great for cooking and warmth. Other wood may be toxic and should be avoided.

Note: Seasoned wood refers to dried wood. Green wood refers to freshly cut wood. Pitch refers to the resin that many coniferous trees excrete.

- Alder: not much heat and a fire burns out quickly, creates good, steady-burning charcoal.

- Apple: Easier to cut when it's green, slow and steady burn when it's dry, not much flame or sparks, good for cooking.

- Ash: Easy to split and saw, produces good heat, burns steady, burns well when it's green and better when it's dry, great wood to burn.

- Beech: Similar properties to ash, fair-burning when it's green, easy to chop, may shoot embers a long distance from the fire.

- Birch: burns unseasoned, burns quickly, produces good heat, rolled up bark pitch can be peeled from trees without causing damage, and is a good firestarter.

- Blackthorn: produces a lot of heat, slow-burning, not much smoke.

- Cedar: produces lasting heat, crackles, and pops when burned, easy to split, best burnt when it's dry but small amounts may be burned unseasoned, good for cooking, no big flames.

- Cherry: produces good heat, slow-burning, slow to start burning, needs to be well seasoned.

- Chestnut: average fuel, not much heat, small flame, shoots embers from the fire.

- Douglas Fir: poor fuel, not much heat, almost no flame.

- Elder: burns quickly, average fuel, produces thick and pungent smoke, not much heat.

- Elm: high water content, fluctuates as fuel, two-year seasoning recommended, may produce a lot of smoke, slow to start burning and may require other wood to get started, slow-burning, splitting isn't easy.

- Eucalyptus: no sparking, contains large amounts of oil and sap when green, fast-burning, not easy to split, eucalyptus scent when burned may not be good for cooking.

- Hawthorn: Good heat production, slow-burning.

- Hazel: fast-burning, needs to be seasoned.

- Holly: can be burned green but better seasoned for one year, good firewood, not much heat, fast-burning, bright flame.

- Hornbeam: similar burn to beech, good heat production, slow-burning.

- Horse Chestnut: poor quality firewood, lots of sparking, good flame.

- Laburnum: toxic, pungent smoke spoils food. Do not use it.

- Larch: average heat production, must be well-seasoned, and crackles.

- Laurel: excellent flame.

- Lime: good for carving, weak flame, low-quality fuel.
- Maple: good as firewood.
- Oak: little flame, pungent smoke unless seasoned for two years. Darkly colored, aged oak produces good great heat, good for cooking, and burns slow and steady.
- Pear: good heat production, must be well-seasoned, no sparking.
- Pine: prone to sparking, must be well-seasoned, good for kindling, great flame.
- Plane: prone to sparking when it's very dry but it burns well.
- Plum: good heat production.
- Poplar: bad fuel, thick and black smoke, does not burn well.
- Rowan: slow-burning, good heat production, good as firewood.
- Rhododendron: Stems that are thick and old burn well.
- Robinia (also known as acacia): pungent smoke, good heat production, slow-burning.
- Spruce: bad firewood, very fast-burning, a lot of sparks.
- Sycamore: average heat production, good flame, cannot be burned green.
- Sweet Chestnut: must be well-seasoned, sparks a lot throughout burning.

- Thorn: slow-burning, excellent heat, great firewood, not much smoke.
- Walnut: variable burning.
- Wellingtonia: bad as firewood.
- Willow: bad firewood, slow-burning, prone to sparking, must be seasoned.
- Yew: intense heat, slow-burning, good for carving.
- The wood you choose for your campfire will depend on what wood is available to you and what the purpose of your fire is.

Which Wood to Burn

Note: Try to always use dry wood as green wood is less effective due to heat loss through evaporation and it produces more smoke which may be harmful.

Hottest Burning Wood

These types of wood are high density with excellent heat production when seasoned, making them the best option when looking for firewood.

- American beech
- Apple
- Ironwood
- Red oak

- Shagbark hickory
- Sugar maple
- White ash
- White oak
- Yellow birch

Medium Burning Wood

These types of wood aren't bad as firewood but obviously are also not the best. They have a medium-density and average heat production when seasoned properly.

- American elm
- Black cherry
- Douglas fir
- Red maple
- Silver maple
- Tamarack
- White birch

Poor Burning Wood

These types of wood should be your last resort when choosing firewood as they are low density and offer poor heat production when properly seasoned.

- Aspen
- Cottonwood

- Hemlock
- Lodgepole pine
- Red alder
- Redwood
- Sitka spruce
- Western red cedar
- White pine

Wood Tips

- When you find suitable, dry wood to use for making a fire, split it and stack it properly to avoid spoiling it.
- Stack the wood off the ground so that it doesn't absorb moisture from the soil.
- Protect the wood from rain.
- Split the wood in varying sizes so that you can maintain your fire level as needed.

Tips for Efficient Wood Burning

It's not always easy to find good wood to burn so it's important to make your burning as efficient as possible. This will result in less wood being used and avoid excessive smoke or loss of heat.

- Use any type of soft wood to start your fire by stacking it in a crisscrossed fashion with a few thin pieces of hardwood on top of the stack. Place tinder in and around the stack.

- Use thin pieces of kindling to get a fire burning more quickly. Thinner pieces of wood will increase the amount of surface area the flames can take hold on.

- To relight a bed of coals, stack them up, instead of spreading them out in a thin layer, and put your kindling on top of the stack.

Avoid Wet Wood

Wherever possible, the use of wet (green) wood should be avoided. The fire won't be as useful and it will produce a lot more smoke.

- The fire will be very difficult to get started and it will take longer.
- It will be harder to keep your fire burning well.
- The fire will produce a greater amount of dense smoke with not much flame.
- Your fire will burn out faster.
- You won't get much heat from the fire.

Finding Seasoned Wood

It doesn't matter where you may be, building a good quality fire is vital to survival and therefore it's important to seek out dry or seasoned wood. There are a few basic ways to gauge whether the wood is suitable for burning.

Avoid wood that is lying on the ground. These pieces of wood soak up moisture through the ground. Even though the wood is no longer a living part of the tree, it's not going to be properly dried. It is particularly important to avoid food on the ground if the weather is or has recently been rainy. Look for branches and sticks higher up that may be broken or dead.

If you find a small enough piece of wood that you can easily snap in your hands, do so. You should hear a loud cracking sound and it should not bend and take effort to snake. Green wood is more flexible and harder to break.

Avoid wood that has a green color to it or that has buds or leaves on it.

If you find a piece of wood that is too large for you to snap it, touch the end of it to your lips. This may not seem like an ideal way to test the wood but you'd be surprised just how sensitive your lips are. Your lips should easily pick up whether the wood still has moisture in it.

Wood to Avoid

Don't be fooled if the wood you're burning has a pleasant scent. You should always try to avoid inhaling smoke from a fire. The chemicals produced when burning wood for a fire are toxic irrespective of what tree it comes from. The particles a fire produces and gives off in smoke are harmful and can leave you with a runny nose, a burning feeling in your eyes, and may even result in making you sick by triggering an asthma attack in asthma sufferers or causing illness like bronchitis.

That being said, there are types of wood that you should avoid burning at all costs because they give off particularly toxic smoke such as yew, elder, and laurel.

- Driftwood is saturated with salt and may release chemicals that are harmful or even toxic.

- Don't burn anything that has 'poison' in its name such as poison oak, poison sumac, poison ivy, etc. Burning these types of wood gives off an oily irritant called urushiol in the smoke which, when inhaled, can cause irritation to your lungs or an intense allergic reaction in your respiratory system.

- Every single part of an oleander shrub is highly toxic and should never be used for any purpose.

- North America alone has more than 20 different species of endangered trees, including American chestnut and blue ash trees. Make sure that you know which trees are endangered and may be growing in the wilderness area you're visiting and how to identify them.

Starting a Fire

Whether you're in an emergency situation or you just want to enjoy bushcraft recreationally, you need to know how to start a fire. There are various ways of starting a fire either with items you have with you, commercial fire starters, or using only natural items from your surroundings.

Starting a Fire Au Natural

Let's take a look at the two most basic methods of starting a fire with only natural items foraged from your surroundings in the wilderness.

Fire Plow

- Find yourself a flat piece of seasoned hardwood that is a couple of inches thick. This will be the base of your fire plow.
- Use your knife to cut a straight groove lengthwise down the center of your base and hollow out the groove to roughly ¼-inch wide.
- Now you need to find a softwood stick that is at least one-inch thick and carve one end of that stick so that it forms a rounded tip that will fit into the groove you just made in your hardwood base.

- Vigorously rub the rounded tip of your softwood stick along the groove in your base. You're going to have to put some elbow grease and force behind your effort.

- Slowly you will see wood shavings coming off the hardwood base. The friction produced from the rubbing will start to make the wood heat up. This will cause tiny embers to form and those embers will ignite the wood shavings.

- Have your tinder close at hand and once enough embers have formed place it in a thin layer on top of the embers. Remember that for the tinder to ignite from the embers, the layer needs to be thin and allow air to reach the embers, otherwise, you're going to smother them. Then you'll have to start the whole process again.

Hand Drill

- For this method, you are going to use softwood. Find a flat piece to use as a baseboard, just like the hardwood base of a fire plow.

- Next, you're going to look for a softwood stick and again carve one end of the stick into a rounded tip.

- Now, cut a little hole in the flat piece of softwood you're using as a base. Cut the hole approximately one inch from the edge of the base and make it only big enough for the rounded tip of your stick to fit in it.

- Cut a triangular wedge into the base so that the point connects with the hole for the stick. The base of the triangle should connect with the other edge of the base.

- Put your tinder into the wedge.

- Put your drill stick into the hole and place your hands on either side of it near the top end. The palms of your hands should be flat and facing each other.

- Press your hands together and rub your hands back and forth against each other to cause the drill stick to rub in the hole.

- Increase the friction between the drill stick and the base by applying a downward force as you roll it.

- Vigorously roll the drill stick between your hands to create embers which will spill down into the triangular wedge where you've placed your tinder.

- When your tinder begins to smolder, gently blow on the embers to help your tinder ignite.

Other Ways to Start a Fire

If you have some other tools available to start a fire, they will save you a lot of effort which could end up increasing your chances of survival in an emergency. There are a few common good fire-starting tools that you should consider keeping in your bushcraft bag.

Matches and Lighters: Possibly the most common way of starting a fire is with the use of matches or a lighter. The problem with matches and lighters is that they aren't suitable for every kind of environment despite the invention of butane lighters and water-resistant matches.

Flint and Striker: Another common method of starting a fire is by using a flint and striker and it is favored by outdoorsmen and bushcraft enthusiasts. You need a flint made of fire steel or a steel alloy and a striker. You can even use the back of your knife as a striker. Strike your flint with your striker to produce sparks that will ignite the tinder. Remember to strike your flint as close to the tinder as possible so that the sparks can reach it easily.

Lenses: Lenses held at an angle will concentrate sunlight into a small point and intensify the heat to heat your tinder to the point that it catches alight. You can use a variety of lenses for this such as your eyeglasses, a magnifying glass, a pair of binoculars, or even a light globe from your car.

Steel Wool and a Battery: This is a good way to start a fire in almost any environment. Touch the positive and negative terminals of a 9V battery to very fine steel wool. This will produce heat and even sparks that will set your tinder alight. You can also use wires to connect your car battery to the steel wool to produce the same effect.

Tinder Ideas

Tinder can be found from various sources. Knowing where to find tinder and what to use is extremely helpful in a survival situation.

- Bark from trees is pretty dry and will ignite.
- Dry lint from your clothing or clothes dryer ignites quickly.
- Cotton balls coated in Vaseline are an old survivalist trick. Petroleum jelly is flammable and the cotton balls will burn easily.
- Natural tinder includes the husks of a coconut, dried leaves and grass, the fluffy material inside cattails, and bird nests but please make sure the nest is not in use.
- As with Vaseline, a piece of petroleum gauze dressing from a first aid kit will ignite readily. Once it's lit, place some other tinder, like dried leaves, on top of it but be careful not to smother the flame.

Keeping a Fire Going

Once you've started your fire, you will want to keep it burning for as long as you can. This is especially true if you are spending the night in the wilderness.

- Use dry or seasoned wood.
- Collect lots of wood so that you can add more wood to the fire as the previous wood starts burning out.
- If possible, use hardwood as it burns longer.
- Feed your fire with oxygen by blowing on it or fanning it with a suitable item such as cardboard.
- Poke the logs around.
- If possible, choose a type of wood that is known to be slow-burning.
- If possible, protect your fire from the elements, such as rain or snow.

Fire Safety

Whether you are recreationally camping or lighting a fire for survival, there are some safety precautions to take into consideration.

- If you don't know how to keep a fire under control, don't build it close to your shelter to prevent sparks or spitting embers from setting your shelter alight, especially in windy conditions.
- Make a small fire from slow-burning wood so that you have a bed of burning coals instead of an open flame.
- Have at least one option for putting your fire out quickly if necessary.
- Pack rocks around your fire, cover them with dirt and remove vegetation surrounding your fire to act as a firebreak to prevent the fire from spreading.
- If you are recreationally camping, always put a fire out before turning in for the night.

Chapter 8:

Be Ready for the

Unexpected

Even seasoned survivalists and outdoorsmen get into tricky situations when spending time out in the wilderness. Whether it's not taking the weather into account or taking the wrong path and getting lost. When you venture out into the wilderness, it is incredibly important that you expect the unexpected and plan accordingly so that you minimize the risk of landing yourself in an emergency situation.

Extreme Cold

Cold weather is responsible for approximately 680 deaths annually which are more casualties than all other extreme weather conditions put together (Jefferson, 2010c). Here are a few ways to make sure that you stay in the loop when it comes to cold weather.

- Access to simple radio communications like an NOAA Weather Radio for extreme weather warnings up to 24 hours in advance.
- Listen to local weather forecasts on an AM/FM radio.
- Pack extra winter gear such as blankets for your trip during cold weather and winter months.

Storm Tips

- Watch the weather and use your senses to pick up on clues about an approaching storm such as a bank of clouds, an increase in wind, and a drop in temperature.
- Summer storms often occur in the afternoon. Head out on a one-day adventure early and return to safety before the time of day that poses the most risk.
- Find shelter.
- If you are on the water, come ashore as quickly as possible.

Extreme Heat

Extreme heat is just as dangerous as extreme cold because of the chances of dehydration, heat exhaustion, heatstroke, etc. Extreme heat accounts for approximately 350 casualties annually (Jefferson, 2010c). It can be difficult to avoid extreme heat and vigilance is important. When the heat strikes, here's how to handle it.

- Seek shade.
- Stay hydrated by drinking around 500ml to one liter (16 to 32 oz) of water per hour.
- Avoid unnecessary tasks.
- Stay out of the direct sun and rest during the hottest part of the day, noon to five PM.
- Wear light-colored clothing that is loose and made of cotton.
- Cool off by soaking clothing and towels in some water.
- Don't use an electric fan as it dries your skin, preventing sweat evaporation.
- Use a misting bottle to spray yourself with water which acts much like sweat to cool you down.

Lightning

Lightning during a storm can pose a very real threat when you are spending time outdoors. Annually it accounts for between 60 and 90 casualties and approximately 500 injuries which is more than hurricanes and tornadoes put together (Jefferson,

2010c). Lightning can be unpredictable as to where and when it may strike. A rule of thumb is that if you can hear the thunder, it's close enough to strike as a bolt of lightning can strike up to 10 miles from the main storm.

- Avoid tall trees or objects.
- Even if you are heading for shelter, don't cross an open area.
- Follow the 30/30 rule by remaining inside the shelter when lightning and thunder occur 30 seconds (or less) apart. Wait 30 minutes before leaving your shelter after the storm has passed.
- Remove all metal items from your person and place them far away.
- If you are camping in a wooded area, stay out of your tent and a fair distance away.
- Find a shelter that has a way to conduct lightning from the roof to the ground such as wiring or plumbing.
- If your shelter is not grounded, the entire thing could become electrically charged.
- Don't come into contact with water.
- If you are in a car, stay inside and keep the windows closed and stay away from the doors.
- Avoid using electronic devices.
- If you are out in the wilderness, avoid hilltops and open areas.

- In forests, avoid tall trees or trees that are standing apart or alone, rather take shelter in a heavily tree-populated area.
- Try to find dry ground.
- If you are caught in an open area, seek out a valley and make yourself as small as possible with the least amount of your body touching the ground such as crouching on the balls of your feet.
- If you are in a group, stand at least 20 feet apart, being huddled together will cause all members of the group to be electrocuted if one person is struck.

Flooding

Flooding accounts for approximately 100 casualties annually (Jefferson, 2010c). Even if the water is rising slowly, don't be deceived. The main reason people are killed during flooding is that they get swept away and drown.

- Don't attempt to drive through a flood current.
- Don't attempt to cross water that is deeper than six inches.
- If you cannot determine the depth, don't cross. Remember that wilderness ground isn't flat,

even if the first few steps are six inches deep, there could be a sudden dip in the ground.

Navigation

Whether you know where you are going or happen to find yourself lost, being able to read a map and use a compass are vital outdoor survival skills. Here are some tips for navigation in the wilderness.

- Learn to effectively read a map. It's somewhat more complicated to read but a Military Grid Reference System map is better to use than a latitude-longitude map. It will take some time and practice but it's worth the time and effort.

- Along with being able to read a map, you should also learn to use a compass. There are various types of compasses on the market.

- Button compass: Often found in cars, good for just getting your bearings and finding direction. Not good for woodland navigation if you don't know where you are or which direction to go in.

- Orienteering compass (mountaineering compass): A magnetic needle points toward the magnetic north. It has a dial that rotates to find direction, median lines that may be oriented according to longitudinal lines on a map, and a travel direction arrow.

- Lensmatic and prismatic compasses: These fall into the category of orienteering compasses but offer additional features such as glow in the dark directional arrows and phosphorous features.

- Declination refers to the difference between magnetic north and true north. Declination changes annually and may vary from an eastern side of a country to the western side of a country. You will need to adjust the declination on your compass regularly.

Common Compass Mistakes

- Metal objects such as bushcraft tools and even zippers or your watch may interfere with your compass.

- Not orienteering your compass to your map to determine your traveling direction.

- Incorrectly holding the compass.

- Keeping your eyes glued to your compass instead of using visual bearing indicators such as landmarks.

- Infrequently checking your bearing.

- Not adjusting your compass for declination.

- Not learning how to read and use a compass properly.

No Map or Compass?

There are five natural navigational techniques that you can lose if you don't have a map or a compass with you or if you've lost them while out in the wilderness. All of these techniques require you to have intimately acquainted yourself with the area you are going to be in so that you know what to look for and what to use as navigational cues. To learn these techniques, have a map handy so that you can follow the instructions with a visual aid.

Handrails are things like trails, roads, pipelines, creeks, etc. that may be followed to reach your destination. They can also be used as backstops.

Backstops are often handrails that are used to tell you when you've strayed too far in a particular direction and need to change your traveling direction.

Baselines are used to help you get back to your starting point. They may be creeks, roads, trails, etc. The only requirements are that they run past your point, are easily visible so that you don't accidentally cross them without realizing it, they are relatively straight, and that they are of significant length. Let's say your starting point is found along a roadway that runs in a general north-south direction and you set out in a north-easterly direction from your camp. You reach your destination but it's not necessarily as easy as simply turning around and heading back. You could easily stray off from your original path of travel or get turned around in circles. From your destination, decide whether you want to travel in a south-south-westerly or north-north-westerly direction. If you were traveling in a north-easterly direction from your camp then as you turn around, the camp will be in a south-westerly direction. Traveling more north or more south of south-west will place camp pretty much between where you will come out on your baseline. If you choose to travel north-north-west then when you reach your baseline you will turn left to reach your camp. If you choose to travel south-south-west, you will turn right when you reach your baseline.

Aiming off refers to picking a direction to travel in from your starting point and using baselines and handrails. This will help you reach your destination and navigate back to your starting point. Let's use that same scenario that your starting point is on a north-south roadway. Your destination is in a north-easterly direction. To the north of your starting point, you will identify a combination handrail. Let's say your handrail is a trail path. To the east of that trail, the path should be another handrail that creates a junction with the path, such as a pipeline, that leads to your destination. If you stray too much to the north and hit the trail, you can turn east and follow the trail to the junction with the pipeline. At the junction you know to turn south and follow the pipeline to your destination. The second handrail you need to identify must create a junction with your baseline and it will help you navigate back to your baseline. Let's say this handrail is a creek that runs in an east-west direction. When you leave your destination to return to the starting point, you will know to travel in a south-westerly direction. If you stray too far south of your starting point and you hit the creek, you know to turn west and follow the creek back to your roadway baseline. As you have been traveling in a more southerly direction to your starting point, you will know to turn north when you hit the roadway and it will lead you back to your starting point.

Blazing refers to marking a natural feature at or near your starting point on a baseline so that when you use the other four techniques to navigate, that marking will indicate that you have come back to your starting point.

As you can see, the first four techniques require you to intimately familiarize yourself with the area and terrain before you even leave home. That way, if you forget or lose your map, you can still make your way to a destination and back to your starting point again.

Finding North Without a Compass

If you don't have a compass and can't accurately tell which way is east and which is west by simply looking at the sun, you can use a shadow cast by the sun to help you find your bearings. If you are trying to navigate at night, you can use the moon and stars to help you find your way.

Shadow Stick Method

- Using a shadow stick requires you to make use of the middle of the day.
- Place a long stick into the ground in a clearing.
- Mark the mark where the tip of the shadow falls.
- Make several more marks as the sun travels through its highest point at midday and then past that point.
- Once you have made several marks and the sun has passed the midday mark, you will use the shortest shadow to indicate north.
- If the moon is bright enough, you can apply this method for nighttime navigation. Use the stick's shadow, making use of the shortest shadow cast by the moon when it is at its highest point in the sky.

Using the Stars

In order to use the stars to navigate you must be able to pick out two constellations, the Big Dipper and the Little Dipper. Each dipper is made up of two parts, a bowl, and a handle.

Draw an imaginary line between the last star in the Big Dipper's bowl and the last star in the Little Dipper's handle, also known as the North Star. This line is known as Polaris and points north from the Big Dipper toward the Little Dipper.

When You're Lost

It's important to know what steps to take when you are lost in the wilderness or even suspect that you may be lost.

- Admit you're not sure where you are. Denial and continuing to blunder on just gets you more lost.

- Remain calm. Panicking clouds your judgment. Think about your movements, whether in a straight line or turning, and what direction you were moving in.

- Be observant and try to find clues that could help you such as which way north is, footprints and the direction they are going in, and visible and recognizable landmarks.

- Place a brightly colored waypoint marker somewhere high up. You can walk in any direction to try to find a familiar area or path as long as you can see the marker and return to it.

- If you have one with you, use a GPS or phone to find your location. If you battle for a signal, use a waypoint marker to move around to find a signal.

- Stay put in the area you got lost, it makes it easier for help to find you if you're as close as possible to where you went off track. Create a shelter, find water, and find food within sight of a waypoint marker.

- If you must, find a higher vantage point which may offer you the sight of a road, town, building, or a recognizable landmark to orientate yourself.

- Look for signs of people and listen for footsteps or voices.

- Find an open space and have a signaling method so that you are visible to rescue planes.

- When the sun sets, stay put. Stumbling around at night is dangerous and could get you turned around in circles without being able to see signs of people or landmarks.

First Aid

When you spend time in the wilderness, some of the most crucial knowledge you must have is first aid. You don't have to be a professional EMT but you need to at least know the basics. Below are some of the most basic first aid skills to learn. It is well worth investing in taking an accredited first aid course so that if worst comes to worst, you have a wider base of knowledge and skills to draw on.

CPR

This is one of the most fundamental skills anybody can learn. CPR stands for cardiopulmonary resuscitation. Even if you took a course a few years ago, you will need to take another one as the standard has changed. The focus is not on chest compressions and leaves out the breathing component. The force of the compressions has also changed to lower the risk of injuring the person you are resuscitating.

Splint Making

A splint immobilizes a broken bone or sprain to speed up recovery and allow movement with significantly less pain. A straight splint can be made by collecting sticks and using some form of binding material wrapped around the limb from pieces of cloth to duct tape. If a sprain is serious or a bone is broken, seek medical attention as soon as possible.

Cleaning and Dressing Wounds

Cleaning wounds effectively will prevent infection which could lead to serious illness and even death. It involves wound irrigation and dressing the wound with a clean covering. Knowing how to close a deep wound with a butterfly stitch is also helpful.

When caring for a wound, this is what to do:

- Wash hands or use alcohol-based hand sanitizer.
- Clear the wound of large debris with sterile tweezers.
- Clean the wound and surrounding area with soap and sterile gauze, avoid pushing debris in.
- Irrigate with purified water.
- Reapply pressure with sterile gauze if the cleaning has restarted bleeding.
- Apply the necessary topical creams and bandages.

Treating Shock

This could save the life of an adventure buddy you may be exploring with. Shock can be a killer in the wilderness and occurs after a traumatic event, perhaps a near-drowning, or a serious injury, such as breaking a bone. Being able to recognize the symptoms of shock allows you to observe them and treat the person such as keeping them calm, keeping them warm or cool to keep their body temperature at the right level, or elevating their feet.

Stemming Bleeding

Being able to stop or control bleeding when out in the wilderness is vital. Large wounds or arterial bleeding could cause death if the bleeding cannot be controlled. Bright red blood is an indication of arterial bleeding. Learning how to apply pressure to slow or stop bleeding and how to bandage the wound properly will help prevent them from losing too much blood. In the case of heavy bleeding, a tourniquet should be your last resort because applied incorrectly could lead to complications or the loss of a limb.

Treating Hypothermia

Hypothermia is a common condition in a survival situation. Without shelter or suitable clothing, cold temperatures can kill you. Recognizing the symptoms of hypothermia could save your life or someone else's.

Signs of hypothermia may develop slowly and can include:

- Shivering which may cease as body temperature gets lower.

- Impaired speech or mumbling.
- Weakened pulse.
- Loss of coordination.
- Breathing becomes slow and shallow.
- Slurred speech or mumbling.
- Slow, shallow breathing.
- Confusion.
- Memory loss.

Treating hypothermia as early as possible is crucial and includes:

- Get out of the cold, protected from wind, insulation from the cold ground.
- Remove and replace wet clothing with warm dry clothes.
- Additional heating in the form of a dry, warm compress, electric blanket, hot water bottles, or hot packs.
- Drink sweet, warm drinks.
- If coughing or shallowly breathing but unresponsive, perform CPR.
- Do not warm the person too fast.
- Don't rewarm the legs or arms, focus on the core.
- No alcohol or cigarettes.

Treating Hyperthermia

Hyperthermia is also called heatstroke and is just as dangerous as hypothermia. Knowing the symptoms could save lives, including your own. Treatment may include increasing your fluid intake, resting in the shade, or placing a damp cloth on the back of your neck to lower your body temperature.

Burn Treatment

Burns can happen even if you are careful. They can be caused by a campfire, touching a hot surface like a kettle, or spilling boiling water on yourself. You may lose several layers of your skin, depending on the severity, leaving you vulnerable to infection which could kill you in a survival situation. You should know how to treat minor, as well as 2nd and 3rd degree burns with first aid supplies. It can be tricky as you need to protect the wound whilst still allowing the wound to breathe and monitoring it carefully.

Again, it cannot be stressed enough how important and advantageous it is to take a credible first aid course, not only for survival situations in the wilderness but also for everyday life.

Conclusion

The basic concepts behind bushcraft are a love of nature, embracing the wilderness, and being well prepared to make the most of a survival situation. It is such a wide topic that covers an immense knowledge base and a vast set of skills that many people have forgotten about. City dwellers, like you, are starting to long to get back in touch with centuries-old ways of experiencing the outdoors and bushcraft is the perfect way to do it.

We have equipped you with a starting point covering some of the basics of bushcraft, including:

- Its history.
- The tools and supplies of the trade.
- How to build your own shelter.
- How to source your own food in the wild.
- The essentials of finding water and starting a fire.
- The basics of expecting and being prepared for various situations that may occur.

With this knowledge, you are already much better equipped to enjoy your time outdoors and increase your chances of survival than the average person who calls the city their home. Now it's time to start practicing those skills and applying that knowledge to gain experience and hone your bushcraft abilities. So, what are you waiting for? You can even start in your own backyard!

Thank you for taking the time to read this book and learn some of the skills that Samuel wants to impart with the world. If you enjoyed reading this book and found it to be an informative insight into the natural world, please leave it a review so that other prospective outdoor enthusiasts can draw on his knowledge as well.

References

Alan. (2016, July 12). *9 most important first aid skills to learn.* Urban Survival Site. https://urbansurvivalsite.com/important-first-aid-skills/

Alexa R. (2019, September 17). *Bushcraft skills checklist: How to survive and thrive in the wilderness when SHTF.* Tactical Blog. https://www.tactical.com/bushcraft-skills-checklist-shtf

Allan, P. (2018, May 18). *How to survive extreme heat in the great outdoors.* Lifehacker. https://lifehacker.com/how-to-survive-extreme-heat-in-the-great-outdoors-1827364107

Anderberg, J. (2016, April 20). *How to find water in the wilderness.* The Art of Manliness. https://www.artofmanliness.com/articles/how-to-find-water-in-the-wild

ASG Staff. (2017, July 13). *Get hooked: DIY survival fish hooks.* American Survival Guide. https://www.asgmag.com/survival-skills/survival-hunting-fishing/get-hooked-diy-survival-fish-hooks

Baltayan, A. (n.d.). *What to do if you get lost in the woods - Find your way without help.* Money Crashers. https://www.moneycrashers.com/5-tips-lost-in-woods/

Boeckmann, C. (2019, December 9). *Animal track identification.* Old Farmer's Almanac. https://www.almanac.com/content/animal-track-identification

Bowen, T. (2017, December 13). *How to source and purify water.* Wildway Bushcraft. https://www.wildwaybushcraft.co.uk/purify-water

Bowen, T. (2018, February 27). *Trapping and snaring.* Wildway Bushcraft. https://www.wildwaybushcraft.co.uk/trapping-snaring

Bowen, T. (2018b, March 6). *How to catch and cook fish in the wild.* Wildway Bushcraft. https://www.wildwaybushcraft.co.uk/catch-cook-fish-wild

Bowline - How to tie a bowline knot animated and step by step illustrated. (n.d.). Www.Netknots.Com. https://www.netknots.com/rope_knots/bowline

Brentza, P. (2017, April 7). *7 Best bushcraft gear to own for survival and preparedness.* Skilled Survival.

https://www.skilledsurvival.com/bushcraft-gear

Bushcraft clothing, what to buy and use? (2015, December 14). The Woodsman - A Bushcraft Blog. https://woodsmanbushcraftblog.wordpress.com/2015/12/14/bushcraft-clothing-what-to-buy-and-use

Bushcraft preparation: Things you need to know before living in the wild. (2018, August 9). Survival Supply Zone. https://blog.survivalsupplyzone.com/skills/bushcraft/living-in-the-wild

Bushcraft: Who, what, when, where, why and how? (n.d.). Www.Parkwoodoutdoors.Co.Uk. https://www.parkwoodoutdoors.co.uk/centre/Dolygaer/News/47/bushcraft-who-what-when-where-why-and-how

Bushcraftbartons. (2011). *Bushcraft: How to make a tool in the bush! [YouTube Video].* On YouTube. https://www.youtube.com/watch?v=x-lKG-TYHbU

Canterbury, J. (2017, September 17). *Best tools to store in your DIY bushcraft camp.* Self Reliance Outfitters. https://www.selfrelianceoutfitters.com/blogs/survival-blog/best-tools-to-store-in-your-diy-bushcraft-camp

Capps, S. (2016, December 27). *How to use a topographic map.* Survival Sullivan.

https://www.survivalsullivan.com/use-topographic-map/

Caudill, C. (2013, July 6). *Bushcraft tracking skills: Animal tracking and man tracking.* How To Survive Stuff. http://www.howtosurvivestuff.com/survival-lifestyle/survival-skills/bushcraft-tracking-skills-animal-tracking-and-man-tracking

Coalcracker Bushcraft. (2019). *Traditional rope making [YouTube Video].* On YouTube. https://www.youtube.com/watch?v=TC_uwEr HOTk

Coalcracker Bushcraft. (2020). *What to do if you are lost in the woods! [YouTube Video].* On YouTube. https://www.youtube.com/watch?v=ZTuBbgr 257s

Combs, D. (2019, July 29). *A Guide to foraging for medicinal plants.* Hobby Farms. https://www.hobbyfarms.com/a-guide-to-foraging-for-medicinal-plants

Cordage making tutorial. (2020). Jonsbushcraft.Com. http://www.jonsbushcraft.com/cordage%20ma king.htm

Curtis, R. (2015). *Guide to animal tracking | Outdoor action.* Princeton.Edu. https://outdooraction.princeton.edu/nature/gu ide-animal-tracking

Dahl, T. (2015, December 3). *The difference between an axe and a hatchet, explained.* Popular Mechanics. https://www.popularmechanics.com/home/to ols/how-to/a18403/whats-the-difference/

Dehydration. (2019). NHS UK. https://www.nhs.uk/conditions/dehydration

Eichenberger, E. W. (2017, February 11). *8 primitive weapons for survival and bushcraft.* Survival Sullivan. https://www.survivalsullivan.com/primitive-weapons-survival-prepping-bushcraft

Essential knots for bushcraft survival and prepping. (2020, April 1). UK Preppers Guide. https://www.ukpreppersguide.co.uk/essential-knots-for-bushcraft-survival-and-prepping

Fagan, S. (n.d.). *The value of partial tracks.* Pioneer Bushcraft. https://www.pioneerbushcraft.org/nature-articles/bushcraft-articles/bushcraft-tracking-partial-tracks

Fenna, J. (2018, February 21). *Bushcraft: Health & safety.* Gun Mart. https://www.gunmart.net/bushcraft/bushcraft-health-safety

Field & Stream Online Editors. (2006, October 17). *Six primitive traps for catching food in the woods.* Field & Stream. https://www.fieldandstream.com/photos/galle

ry/kentucky/2006/10/six-primitive-traps-catching-food-woods

Five W's shelter checklist | Bushcraft spirit. (n.d.). Www.Bushcraftspirit.Com. http://www.bushcraftspirit.com/five-w-shelter-checklist

Foraging 101: Where to find your bounty. (2018, August 28). Chelsea Green Publishing. https://www.chelseagreen.com/2018/foraging-101-where-to-forage

Foraging Guide - Month by month. (n.d.). Woodland Trust. https://www.woodlandtrust.org.uk/visiting-woods/things-to-do/foraging

Gary. (2016, March 22). *Finding water in the outdoors.* Jack Raven Bushcraft. https://www.jackravenbushcraft.co.uk/finding-water

Gary. (2019, June 2). *What makes good firewood?* Jack Raven Bushcraft. https://www.jackravenbushcraft.co.uk/what-makes-good-firewood

Geek Adventures. (n.d.). *Leave no trace, what it is and why it's important.* Camping Rentals. https://camping.rentals/leave-no-trace/

Guy, G. (2019, April 25). *Top 5 bushcraft skills you need to know.* Outdoor Revival.

https://www.outdoorrevival.com/old-ways/top-5-bushcraft-skills-you-need-to-know.html

Hendry, K. (2015, October 5). *Bushcraft tools must haves.* Survival Sullivan. https://www.survivalsullivan.com/bushcraft-tools-must-haves

Hendry, K. (2016, March 16). *15 Wild edible plants: How to identify, harvest and eat them.* Survival Sullivan. https://www.survivalsullivan.com/15-wild-edible-plants-identify-harvest

Hendry, K. (2016, January 11). *Top 6 safest water purification methods for survival.* Survival Sullivan. https://www.survivalsullivan.com/water-purification-methods

Haynes, H. (2015, July 14). *14 Bushcraft essentials.* Heinnie Haynes. https://heinnie.com/blog/14-bushcraft-essentials

How to skin and gut an animal. (n.d.). Alpha Outpost. https://www.alphaoutpost.com/blogs/alpha-outpost-the-only-subscription-box-that-keeps-you-prepared-for-any-situation/how-to-skin-and-gut-an-animal

Hubbard, J. (n.d.). *Video: How to make a splint.* The Survival Doctor. http://thesurvivaldoctor.com/2011/12/06/video-how-to-make-a-splint/

Huffstetler, E. (2014, October 1). *Printable foraging journal.* Www.Myfrugalhome.Com. https://www.myfrugalhome.com/printable-foraging-journal

Hunter, J. (2020, January 7). *5 ridiculously simple animal traps and snares for outdoor survival.* Primal Survivor. https://www.primalsurvivor.net/simple-animal-traps-snares

Hunting techniques. (n.d.). Www.Alimentarium.Org. https://www.alimentarium.org/en/knowledge/hunting-techniques

Introduction to animal tracking: An ancient skill for reading the stories of wildlife. (2017, November 14). Nature Mentoring. https://nature-mentor.com/introduction-to-animal-tracking

Jefferson, J. (2010a, December 14). *Stay dry – The first rule of survival.* Survival Cache. https://survivalcache.com/hypothermia-survival-stay-dry-survival-gear

Jefferson, J. (2010b, February 5). *Best fire starters for survival in 2020: Hands-on reviews, and ways to make fire.* Survival Cache. https://survivalcache.com/survival-fire-starters

Jefferson, J. (2010c, June 23). *Weather preparedness part 1: The top 4 killers.* Survival Cache. https://survivalcache.com/weather-survival/

Jefferson, J. (2010d, March 10). *5 ideas for fire tinder.* Survival Cache. https://survivalcache.com/fire-tinder

Jefferson, J. (2010e, March 4). *7 great uses for a backpacking bucket.* Survival Cache. https://survivalcache.com/collapsible-bucket

Jefferson, J. (n.d.). *4 types of base camps and when to use them.* Survival Cache. https://survivalcache.com/survival-base-camp-types

John. (2016, May 8). *Animal tracking.* Wildway Bushcraft. https://www.wildwaybushcraft.co.uk/animal-tracking/

Johnston, N. (2011, August 2). *15 wild plants you can eat.* Outdoor Canada. https://www.outdoorcanada.ca/15-wild-plants-you-can-eat

Jones, B. (2018, August 3). *A beginner's guide to finding wild edible plants that won't kill you.* Popular Science. https://www.popsci.com/find-wild-edible-plants

Kirtley, P. (2013). *Bushcraft - Essential winter fire lighting techniques* [YouTube Video]. On YouTube. https://www.youtube.com/watch?v=Ld3e01dP7CA

Kirtley, P. (2013). *How to pack your bushcraft camping gear into a rucksack [YouTube Video]*. On YouTube. https://www.youtube.com/watch?v=WGlfnvp xE_c

Kirtley, P. (2016, October 12). *Getting started with bushcraft: Kit considerations for beginners*. Paul Kirtley. http://paulkirtley.co.uk/2016/getting-started-with-bushcraft-kit-considerations-for-beginners/

Kjermsmo, K. (1997). *How to use a compass - When you have no compass....* Www.Learn-Orienteering.Org. https://www.learn-orienteering.org/old/nocompass1.html

Lambert, C. (2019, May). *Five of the greatest wilderness survival stories in history*. The Clymb. https://blog.theclymb.com/passions/history-2/five-of-the-greatest-wilderness-survival-stories-in-history/

Lucasbosch. (2011, November 5). *Deutsch: doppelter schotstek, unsichere versionEnglish: Double sheet bend knot, unsecure version*. Wikimedia Commons. https://commons.wikimedia.org/wiki/File:Dou ble_sheet_bend.svg

MacWelch, T. (2017, May 8). *5 clues for tracking wild animals besides tracks*. Outdoor Life. https://www.outdoorlife.com/5-clues-for-tracking-wild-animals-besides-tracks

MacWelch, T. (2019, October 21). *A guide to the 15 best survival traps of all time.* Outdoor Life. https://www.outdoorlife.com/how-build-trap-15-best-survival-traps

MacWelch, T. (2020, June 29). *Nine traits of the survival mindset that will keep you calm in regular life and life-threatening situations.* The Budd Group. https://www.buddgroup.com/nine-traits-of-the-survival-mindset-that-will-keep-you-calm-in-regular-life-and-life-threatening-situations/

Mayo Clinic Staff. (2020, April 15). *Hypothermia: First aid.* Mayo Clinic. https://www.mayoclinic.org/first-aid/first-aid-hypothermia/basics/art-20056624

McCarthy, A. (2015, May 28). *Foraging 101: 5 rules for finding wild foods.* Pastemagazine.Com. https://www.pastemagazine.com/food/foraging-101-5-rules-for-finding-your-food

McCarthy, P. (2017, October 15). *Survival trapping: 4 easy traps to learn.* Recoil Offgrid. https://www.offgridweb.com/survival/survival-trapping-4-easy-traps-to-learn

McKay, B., & McKay, K. (2010, October 6). *Edible wild plants: 19 wild plants you can eat to survive in the wild.* The Art of Manliness. https://www.artofmanliness.com/articles/surviving-in-the-wild-19-common-edible-plants

Mills, C., Horkavy, K., & Hochhaus, R. (2019, October 19). *Why do people enjoy bushcraft and living in the wilderness?* Www.Quora.Com. https://www.quora.com/Why-do-people-enjoy-bushcraft-and-living-in-the-wilderness

Monthei, A. (2019, April 24). *The beginner's guide to fishing.* Outside Online. https://www.outsideonline.com/2393713/how-to-start-fishing

Monthly foraging guide: What's in season, where to find it, and how to forage responsibly. (n.d.). Countryfile.Com. https://www.countryfile.com/how-to/foraging/monthly-foraging-guide-whats-in-season-where-to-find-it-and-how-to-forage-responsibly

Nick, J. (2018, May 15). *8 kinds of wood that you should absolutely never burn.* Good Housekeeping. https://www.goodhousekeeping.com/home/a20705861/kinds-of-wood-not-to-burn

Peterson, D. (2011, August 30). *30 uses for rope or paracord.* Survival Camping Store.Com. http://www.survivalcampingstore.com/30-Uses-For-Rope-Or-Paracord_b_32.html

Phyzome. (2008, April 25). *Make rope out of dead plants -- With no tools.* Instructables. https://www.instructables.com/id/Make-rope-out-of-dead-plants----with-no-tools

Pinkerton, P. (2016, September 12). *Burning the right wood in your campfire - it makes all the difference.* Outdoor Revival. https://www.outdoorrevival.com/adventure/burning-the-right-wood-in-your-campfire-it-makes-all-the-difference.html

Portable water filter. (n.d.). BushcraftLab. https://www.bushcraftlab.co.uk/collections/portable-water-filter

Quiñonez, J. P. (2017, June 23). *Best 6 primitive survival fish traps (How to).* Survival Skills Guide. https://survivalskills.guide/best-primitive-survival-fish-traps-how-to

Reynolds, M. (2012, July 31). *Which wood is best for firewood? Tips for eco-friendly heat.* Www.Ecohome.Net. https://www.ecohome.net/guides/2322/burning-the-right-firewood

Rob. (2020, January 16). *Bushcraft essentials List - A complete kit.* Pursuing Outdoors. https://pursuingoutdoors.com/bushcraft-essentials-list/#Bushcraft_Essentials_List_8211_Clothing

Ruiz, C. (2015, March 12). *Bushcraft skills: Foraging for food.* The Bug Out Bag Guide. https://www.thebugoutbagguide.com/bushcraft-skills-foraging

Seitz, D. (2020, February 5). *How to find drinkable water in the wild.* Popular Science. https://www.popsci.com/story/diy/find-drinkable-water-wild

Sheet bend - weaver's knot | Animated and illustrated. (n.d.). Www.Netknots.Com. https://www.netknots.com/rope_knots/sheet-bend

Square knot - How to tie a square knot. (2018). Netknots.Com. https://www.netknots.com/rope_knots/square-knot

Stewart, M. (2015, December 8). *How to use a compass.* Survival Sullivan. https://www.survivalsullivan.com/how-to-use-a-compass/

Stewart, M. (2015, July 9). *How to find water in the wilderness.* Survival Sullivan. https://www.survivalsullivan.com/how-to-find-water

Stewart, M. (2015, November 9). *The best EDC (everyday carry) knives.* Survival Sullivan. https://www.survivalsullivan.com/the-best-edc-everyday-carry-knives

Strider. (2020, June 23). *Primitive hunting techniques.* Survival Gear Book.

https://survivalgearbook.com/primitive-hunting-techniques

Sullivan, D. F. (2015, June 27). *Literally every way to start a fire.* Survival Sullivan. https://www.survivalsullivan.com/literally-every-way-to-start-a-fire-and-keep-it-going-afterwards

Sullivan, D. F. (2015, November 20). *21 survival shelters you should learn how to make.* Survival Sullivan. https://www.survivalsullivan.com/how-to-make-a-shelter

Survival Sherpa. (2016, April 18). *How to build a river cane fish trap [YouTube Video].* On YouTube. https://www.youtube.com/watch?v=3Rq9MtKQHNo

Survival Stories. (2018, September 9). Bushcraft Buddy. https://bushcraftbuddy.com/survival-stories/

TA Outdoors. (2017). *10 knots for bushcraft & camping - How to tie knots | Shed Sunday EP. 3 [YouTube Video].* On YouTube. https://www.youtube.com/watch?v=ThCMrTY5dsc

The Survival Enthusiast. (2016, April 28). *Easy animals to hunt.* My Survival Forum. https://mysurvivalforum.com/threads/easy-animals-to-hunt.444

TheElvenArcher. (2017). *How to: 4 simple tarp shelters [YouTube Video]*. On YouTube. https://www.youtube.com/watch?v=S6PhHMi mgxU

Thoms, G. (n.d.). *Bushcraft fishing, what do you really need*. Bushcraftandoutdoors.Com. https://bushcraftandoutdoors.com/bushcraft-fishing-what-do-you-really-need

Tips for surviving a storm while outdoors. (n.d.). Adirondack.Net. https://www.adirondack.net/camping/storm-tips/

Tirman, S. (2017, April 21). *The 8 survival skills every man should know*. Hi Consumption. https://hiconsumption.com/basic-survival-skills-every-man-should-know

Top 5 best bushcraft tarp shelter review & setup tips. (2019, August 16). Survival Supply Zone. https://blog.survivalsupplyzone.com/skills/bushcraft/top-5-bushcraft-tarp-shelter

Types of wood you should not burn in your fireplace. (2017, January 6). Bolt Insurance. https://www.boltinsurance.com/types-of-wood-you-should-not-burn-in-your-fireplace

Unknown. (2012, June 20). *Wood trekker: So, why bushcraft?* Wood Trekker.

http://woodtrekker.blogspot.com/2012/06/so
-why-bushcraft.html

Van Schyndel, N. (n.d.). *Wilderness survival stories archives.*
Survival   Skills   Guide.
https://survivalskills.guide/category/long-
term-wilderness-survival-stories/

Vuković, D. (2016, June 30). *Should you take a wilderness
survival   course?*   Primal   Survivor.
https://www.primalsurvivor.net/wilderness-
survival-course/

What wood to burn. (n.d.). Www.Thestoveyard.Com.
https://www.thestoveyard.com/resource-
centre-home/what-wood-to-burn

Wikibooks, J. at E. (2006, July 28). *English: Illustration of
tying a bowline knot.* Wikimedia Commons.
https://commons.wikimedia.org/wiki/File:Kno
t_bowline.jpg

Wikibooks, J. at E. (2006b, July 28). *English: Illustration of
tying a square knot.* Wikimedia Commons.
https://commons.wikimedia.org/wiki/File:Kno
t_square.jpg

WikiHow Writers. (2019, December 6). *How to skin a
dead   animal.*   WikiHow.
https://www.wikihow.com/Skin-a-Dead-
Animal

WikiHow Writers. (2020, July 2). *How to hunt*. WikiHow. https://www.wikihow.com/Hunt

Wikipedia Contributors. (2019, September 22). *Leave no trace*. Wikipedia. https://en.wikipedia.org/wiki/Leave_No_Trac e

Wild foods you can forage and where to find them. (n.d.). Wild Edible. https://www.wildedible.com/foraging

Wilderness Arena. (2015, May 14). *Animal tracking and signs guide – how to track any animal (even people)*. Wilderness Arena. https://www.wildernessarena.com/overviews/a nimal-tracking-signs-guide

Wilderness survival - 10 tips for surviving in the wild. (2017, October 13). The Real Survivalists. https://therealsurvivalists.com/10-tips-for-surviving-in-the-wild

Wilderness survival shelter designs: How to build one. (2018, September 14). Survival Supply Zone. https://blog.survivalsupplyzone.com/skills/bus hcraft/wilderness-survival-shelter-designs

Wilderness water | Bushcraft Spirit. (n.d.). Www.Bushcraftspirit.Com. http://www.bushcraftspirit.com/wilderness-water

Wood carving tools: Whittling knives, chisels, hand tools. (n.d.).
Www.Woodcraft.Com.
https://www.woodcraft.com/categories/carvin
g-tools#

Wound care: A guide to practice for healthcare professionals.
(2019, November 11). Www.Ausmed.Com.
https://www.ausmed.com/cpd/guides/wound-
care

Made in the USA
Las Vegas, NV
30 October 2020

10448155R00118